Wejee's
Eclectic Book of Shadows

An Encyclopedia of Magical Herbs,
Wiccan Spells and Natural Magic.
A Guide for the Solitary Practitioner, Green
Witch, Wicca Beginners and Adepts Alike.

*By Raven Starhawk Cunningham
and Dr. Jane Ma'ati Smith C.Hyp. Msc.D.*

**Wejee's
Eclectic Book of Shadows**
An Encyclopedia of Magical Herbs,
Wiccan Spells and Natural Magic.
A Guide for the Solitary Practitioner, Green Witch,
Wicca Beginners and Adepts Alike.

*By Raven Starhawk Cunningham
and Dr. Jane Ma'ati Smith C.Hyp. Msc.D.*

ISBN # 1434849503
ISBN –13/EAN13 # 9781434849502

Copyright © 2008 No part of this book may be reproduced in any manner, including internet usage, without written permission from Dr. Jane Ma'ati Smith Msc.D. Brief quotes embodied in critical articles, reviews and affiliate promotions are permitted.

*I Agree to Use
Magick & Herbs*

Safely and Responsibly!

Every effort has been made to provide accurate information in this book. However, due to differing conditions, individual skills and tools, the authors and publisher can not be responsible for any injuries, losses or damages which may result from the information provided in this book. By reading this book, you agree to do magick and use herbs at your own risk! And if you have a serious medical condition, please consult with a qualified medical practitioner before using any information provided in this book.

)O(

We would like to thank and acknowledge all of the spiritual masters and mistresses that have inspired us so deeply, and done so much to bring the practice of Wiccan and Natural Magic into the 21st Century: Scott Cunningham, Silver Ravenwolf, D.J. Conway, Laurie Cabot, Edain McCoy, Raven Grimassi, Patricia Telesco, Starhawk, Raymond Buckland, Gerina Dunwich, Stewart and Janet Farrar, Christopher Penczak, Ann Moura, Dorothy Morrison Ashleen O'Gaea, and many more.

We would also like to acknowledge and honor the masters and mistresses of the other spiritual traditions that have inspired this book: Ted Andrews, Drunvalo Melchizedek, Michael Harner, Doreen Virtue, J. Philip Newell, John Michael Greer, Isaac Bonewits, Jean Markale, Masaru Emoto, Jean Shinoda Bolen, Carlos Castaneda, Black Elk, Caroline Myss, Cassandra Eason, Eckhart Tolle, Rhonda Byrne, Jane Roberts, Nicki Scully, Paramahansa Yogananda, the Dalai Lama and so man more!

And of course, we would like to thank those who have helped from the spirit realm: Thoth, Saraswati, Ganesha, St. Germain, Abraham and Seth, Isis and Quan Yin, Merlin, Gandalf, and the Native Spirits resident in our own personal vortex!

And of course, the enlightened customers of www.wejees.com!

Table of Contents

    Introduction...7
    What is Wicca?...7
    The Wiccan Rede...9
ENERGY- Your Aura, Chakras and Universal Energies...11
    It's all about Energy...12
    The Basic Laws of Universal Energy... 13
    What is synchronicity?...14
    How do you distinguish synchronicity and premonition from wishful thinking? ...16
    Your Aura and Chakras... 16
    Aura... 16
    Aura Colors... 17
    Chakras... 18
    Magickal Balance... 23
    Zhang Fu theory, chakras and "cellular memory"...25
    The Seven Chakras, related organs and illnesses ...25
    Meditation... 28
    Five Pointed Star Meditation... 28
    Sacred Tree Meditation... 29
    A More Advanced Meditation... 30
    Reiki... 40
    Reiki Symbols... 41
    methods for Reiki Symbol activation... 46
    Psychic Protection... 47
    Keeping Yourself Grounded... 47
    Beings Without Bodies... 48
    Breathing...50
    Dreaming...51
    Common Dream Elements, and what they might mean... 52
CORRESPONDENCES- Planetary, Elemental, Gender, Oils, Herbs and Stones... 57
    Basic Correspondences... 58
    What are correspondences?... 58
    Gender...58
    Elemental... 58
    Planetary... 60

Daily Correspondences...61
Moon Phase correspondences...62
Herbal correspondences...64
Why Are Herbs Used In Magick?...64
Ways to use Herbs...64
LIST OF 117 HERBS...65
Essential Oils and Incense... 108
List of 35 Essential Oils... 109
Uses of Common Incense... 116
Crystals and Stones... 117
Clearing and Programming Crystals... 117
Crystals and the Zodiac... 118
Metaphysical Properties of 50 Crystals... 119
Colors... 124
Trees... 127

A SAMPLING OF SIMPLE SPELLS for love, money and protection... 135

Prophetic Dream Pillow... 137
A few words on Soul Mates... 137
Love Attraction Spell... 138
Flower Power Love Spell... 139
Soul Mate Attraction... 142
Heal the Hurt of Lost Love... 143
A few words on Prosperity... 146
Money Attraction Spell... 147
Money Tree Prosperity Spell... 148
Find a Job Spell... 151
Wishing Well Spell... 152
Find a New Home Spell... 153
Keep the Peace Spell... 154
Protection Spell... 155
Mirror Protection Spell... 157
Prosperity Bath Salts... 159
Love Bath Salts... 159

Wejee's
Eclectic Book of Shadows

An Encyclopedia of Magical Herbs, Wiccan Spells and Natural Magic. A Guide for the Solitary Practitioner, Green Witch, Wicca Beginners and Adepts Alike.

*By Raven Wolf-Cunningham
and Dr. Jane Ma'ati Smith C.Hyp. Msc.D.*

Introduction

Wiccan magick utilizes the forces and elements of nature to bring about magickal change, and the power of your own will and spirit is, in itself, the greatest potential force of nature available to you. This indispensable book can serve as an easy reference for both novice and adept alike, a portable 'Book of Shadows', with extensive correspondence charts for 117 herbs, 35 essential oils, 50 crystals and gemstones, 18 varieties of incense, colors, days, and moons, plus thirteen potent spells you can perform for love, prosperity, protection, and more.

Spell ingredients alone will do with little without the right frame of mind, and a certain amount of spiritual development. In addition to Wiccan correspondences and spells, this book also provides vital and eclectic information on the chakras, the aura, meditation, dreams and metaphysics to help you in the development of your most valuable magickal tool- yourself! Easy yet powerful exercises drawn from both the Eastern and Western esoteric traditions will help ground you in the reality where magick happens- in the here and now!

What is Wicca?

Wicca is a peaceful modern day religion, based on the pre-Christian European religion, particularly that of the Celtic British Isles. It is a balanced and natural way of life, fostering a oneness with the Earth, the Divine, and the Universe. Many modern day Wiccans also draw on the spiritually transforming, esoteric traditions of Eastern metaphysics, and resonate with the natural spirit of indigenous peoples in their respect for Mother Earth.

Witchcraft in ancient Europe was the practice of shamans- 'medicine' men and women who worked with the forces of nature on all levels. They had extensive knowledge of herbs and medicine, they acted as oracles, gave counsel, and were the spiritual leaders of their people. They possessed the metaphysical understanding that man is not superior to Nature, but simply one part of a whole; a whole comprised of many levels, both seen and unseen, material and ethereal.

Modern Wicca was created by Gerald Gardner (1884-1964), a British civil servant, who spent much of his career in Southeast Asia. An intelligent and curious man, Gardner was an enthusiastic researcher of folklore, and archeology in the colonial outposts where he served. Gardner believed that folk magick in Great Britain were the remnants of pre-Roman, and possibly even the pre-Celtic religion of Western Europe. When he returned to England permanently, shortly before World War II, he devoted himself entirely to research of the occult, and of 'the old religion'. During his research, he claimed to have encountered members of a secret group called 'The Wica'. He

found the witchcraft practiced by the Wicans spiritually rich, and he devoted the remainder of his life to its preservation and propagation. He stated he believed the Wicans were the last living and practicing descendants of the pre-Christian and pre-Roman European religion. Under Gardner's guidance, the group slowly grew, in secrecy, as 'witchcraft' was still illegal in Britain. In 1951 the Witchcraft Laws were replaced by the Fraudulent Mediums Act, and Gerald Gardner went public, actively promoting his new 'old' religion. He won many followers, and his association with Raymond Buckland spread Wicca across the Atlantic to the United States and Canada.

Over the last fifty years, Wicca has grown in many directions, and allows for much individuality. Many follow the Celtic path originally laid out by Gardner, but many others who also identify as Wiccans follow Egyptian teachings, Nordic traditions, and even Native American ways. Many Wiccans also study the esoteric, Eastern metaphysical philosophies of Buddhism, Hinduism, and Sufism- they possess the metaphysical understanding that it's all simply one part of a whole; a whole comprised of many levels, both seen and unseen, material and ethereal.

The Wiccan Rede

Bide the Wiccan Laws we must
in perfect love and perfect trust.

Live and let live
fairly take and fairly give.

Cast the Circle thrice about
to keep the evil spirits out.

To bind the spell every time
let the spell be spoke in rhyme.

Soft of eye and light of touch
speak little, listen much.

When ye have a truthful need
hearken not to other's greed.

With a fool no season spend

lest ye be counted as his friend.

Merry meet and merry part
bright the cheeks and warm the heart.

Mind the Threefold Law you should
three times bad and three times good.

Eight words the Wiccan Rede fulfill
An ye harm none, do what ye will.

ENERGY

**Your Aura, Chakras
and Universal Energies**

ENERGY

Your Aura, Chakras and Universal Energies

It's all about Energy

Physics is a science that studies the interactions between matter and energy; the prefix "meta" indicates that which goes beyond or transcends- thus, "metaphysics" is the esoteric study of the interaction between energy and matter. It is the very basis of the art we call Magick- the use of energy to effect the material world.

The physical, material world is made up of atoms and molecules, held together with energy. The nonphysical world of thoughts, emotions and spirit is made of pure energy- it is, in fact, part of a web of energy that holds our perceived reality together. It seems logical then, that if your spirit, thoughts and emotions are part of the web of energy that forms the cohesiveness of reality, that it must then have some effect on it. It does- our thoughts and emotions form our individual and collective reality, through the medium of spiritual energy. The trick is, using this energy to create the reality you want!

The first thing you must understand about creating truly effective magick is this- "As Below, So Above". This means that the reality you create in your outer world is a reflection of your inner world, both conscious and unconscious. Attempting to create magick with an underlying energy of turmoil, heart break, ego or anger will ultimately bring only more of the same, to not only you, but to those around you. The substance of the Universe is composed of energy; a thought, firmly pressed into this 'substance', with the power of desire and the energy of emotion to feed it, will sprout and grow, like a seed.

All religions have certain spiritual 'Laws', designed to aid their followers in leading more fulfilling lives. We, as individuals, may or may not agree with the 'Laws' of particular religions, but the root of this tradition is important; the world we live in is comprised of energy (to the religious, God), and this energy responds to our thoughts, our actions, and our emotions, thus creating our individual and common reality. Learning the metaphysical laws by which this energy operates is not only essential to creating effective magick, but to creating an effective and magickal life!

The Basic Laws of Universal Energy

#1- The energy of the Universe responds to our thoughts, both conscious and unconscious, to create our reality. Thus, the first step to creating the reality we want is to align the thoughts of our conscious and unconscious minds with the vision of our desire. Our unconscious mind is not as "unconscious" and hard to access as we'd like to believe- the running dialog we carry on with ourselves, and the sometimes disturbing and intrusive thoughts we push away is our unconscious mind speaking to us, and making its feelings and beliefs known to us. Acknowledge and accept these thoughts, and if they are not aligned with the reality you want to create, don't fight them; instead simply acknowledge them and lovingly release them, allowing the vision you want to grow and take hold.

#2- This Universal energy is *creative*, not *competitive*. The purpose of this energy is to ultimately *create more life*. In order to align yourself with this energy, you must also pass from the competitive to the creative, creating more life for all. No one has to lose in order for you to win; work your magick and live your life so that all will win! Give more than you receive, knowing in your heart the Universal energy will always create more for all.

#3- The Universal energy resonates with the frequency of *Love and Gratitude*. Resonating with the frequency of love and gratitude aligns you with the frequency of the Universal energy, keeping you within the realm of the creative mind. Nurture the seeds you plant within the Creative Mind with love and gratitude, and the Universal energy will grow your vision.

#4- It's ironic, *but the desires you focus most intensely on will often be the most difficult to manifest.* This is because mental and emotional *obsessions* come from a place of *'want'*, and the Universe will respond to the deepest, most underlying emotions powering your desire. *Want* and *need* have a tendency to keep your dreams just out of reach, like the proverbial 'brass ring' on a Merry Go Round. Feel that you *have*, not that you *want,* and nurture a deep sense of gratitude to the Powers that Be for the continual, unfolding manifestation of your dream. Letting go of mental and emotional obsessions will free your spirit to create on many magickal levels!

#5- The Universal Mind works to create through the everyday channels of reality (which is really the energetic 'construct' created by everyone's combined thoughts, emotions, and energy). Open the channels of Universal energy to flow in your direction by actively working within everyday reality to manifest your dreams. It's all about finding the energetic 'flow'. The flow of the Universe is known as "synchronicity".

What is Synchronicity?

"Synchronicity" is a term coined by the great psychologist C.G. Jung for "meaningful coincidence", events that seemingly have no causal relationship, but are in fact related on a higher plane of meaning. Have you ever thought of someone, only to run into that person later in the day? Or perhaps you narrowly avoided an accident, by turning the corner at just the right time? Synchronicity happens constantly, but most of us only notice the most obvious instances. Nothing is really a coincidence, and the trail of synchronicity can lead you to meet the right people or find things, be in the right place, at the right time, which is really very magickal! How can this be done?

#1- Pay attention to what is going on around you, in a state of peace, *without analyzing, judging, or becoming emotionally involved!* Your 'inner critic' often dismisses synchronicity, because it doesn't seem logical, it's unexpected, or the person or place presented doesn't meet your own preconceived expectations or emotional desires.

#2- Learn to know the difference between premonition and wishful thinking. Is your urge to go to a certain place motivated by preconceived desires or obsessions- "my ex often goes to that park, I think I'll go to the park" (with the secret hope you'll *"accidentally"* run into him?) Real synchronicity would be the park keeps popping into your mind, for no apparent reason or ulterior motives. You go, and maybe you meet no one, but it was nice to get outside, and you feel renewed. Or, maybe you meet an old coworker from an old job, someone you hadn't even thought of, who gives you a lead for a new job.... which leads you to meet new people, which leads you to meet your true soul mate, perhaps months later.

#3- Listen to your body. Our psychic sense is filtered through our *bodies*, not our *minds or emotions*. Calm your mind, still your emotions, and listen to your *body*. Are you feeling an 'energy pull' from any of your chakras? Or an 'energy push'? Try following it, to see what you find, and keep track of the results; you may find patterns which you can begin to use in the interpretation of these sensations. E.S.P.- extra-*sensory* perception- is the natural, instinctive interpretation of the sensory data we are receiving all the time, on all levels. Stop talking to yourself in your head, stop craving with your emotions, and begin to listen to your body and environment for the answers you need.

#4- Understand that the trip is half the fun! The results of your magickal workings most likely will not land neatly in your lap. What is most likely to happen is that the *intent* you put into your magick will subtly change the energetic flow around you- so the message is, go with the flow! Recognize and follow the trail of synchronicity that has magickally opened before you.

How do you distinguish synchronicity and premonition from wishful thinking?

Wishful thinking is generally accompanied by a feeling of anxiety or a craving, the thoughts keep popping into your head, but there is an intrusive, addictive quality to it. You get the feeling you should go somewhere or do something, but are mentally planning on some level what you would like to happen, related to a needy desire. You want something specific to happen, and are semi-consciously scanning for an opening.

Synchronicity and premonition is generally accompanied by a sense of calm, of mindlessness, a feeling that you should follow your heart, but really don't know why. The path is opened by honest desires, those that will lead you to develop your true highest self. We are all born with certain innate talents, with certain spiritual goals, and the path to real, beneficial magick relies on self knowledge. Synchronicity might lead us to people and places we've never even dreamed of, for reasons we can't even imagine. But finding that path is the key to leading a truly magickal life!

Your Aura and Chakras

Your **Aura** is the energy produced by your spirit, it is your 'spiritual body', and it emanates all around you. Your aura is a very sensitive and vital part of your well being, both mentally and physically- you must learn to care for it. Practicing good spiritual 'hygiene' is as important to your well being as good physical hygiene! Our auras can pick up the energy of our environment, other people, and of our society and culture. Often, this energy finds its way into our thoughts, emotions, and even into our physical bodies, affecting our health. Developing and gaining control of your aura is a key to gaining control of your own personal power, and success in your magickal workings!

Your mental, emotional and physical well being is reflected in the colors of your aura. With practice, you can learn to see auras- starting with your own. In a darkened room, lay back and relax, clearing your mind of chatter. Unfocus your eyes, and gaze at your hand- your aura will look like a fuzzy light layer, about half an inch or so from your skin. Do not concentrate on it; like so many things spiritual, too much focus and mental thought will cause you to lose sight of what you seek!

As you gain the ability to see your own aura, you will gradually begin to discern different colors. You can also use the same technique to see the auras of others. Sometimes, if you do not actually see the aura, you will still get an impression of a color, as a picture in your mind's eye, or as a stray thought. You can also consciously alter the color of your aura through meditation on that color, to aid in the healing of your emotions and spirit. *(Please read the section on meditation for this technique).*

AURA COLORS

PURPLE indicates pure spirituality. Purple only appears as flames and flashes, since truly spiritual thoughts only come as flashes and flames of pure, inspired consciousness.

BLUE indicates a person leading a balanced existence, one who feels at ease and is stress free. Blue is a very desirable color for an aura. Blue flashes can also indicate when a person is receiving or sending clairvoyant communication.

TURQUOISE indicates a very dynamic person, very energetic and capable of influencing others. These people are very organized and goal oriented. They make fantastic managers, and are generally very popular with their employees.

GREEN is restful, a natural healing energy. All healers should have green auras. Just being around a person with a strong green aura feels restful and healing. These folks also have a green thumb, and can make anything grow.

YELLOW is a joyful color, the color of a true free spirit. These people are very generous- they are not attached to anything. A yellow halo is a sign of a true spiritual teacher- Jesus, Buddha and the saints all had large, bright yellow auras. It indicates a person who has found enlightenment.

ORANGE is a sign of a desire for power, and to control other people. It can also be inspiring, and can contribute to a yellow halo for a person who has a strong spiritual inclination. Spiritual leaders have this combination.

RED is the color of a person who is preoccupied with their physical body, and whos thoughts dwell on material desires.

CHAKRAS

Chakra is a Sanskrit word meaning "spinning wheel of energy". These energy centers within our bodies receive and transmit energy, and each is situated at a major endocrine gland, and nerve bundle within the physical body, called a plexus. Each chakra is connected and associated with a different part of the body. There are seven chakras. Each chakra has a color, and different gemstones and crystals can be associated with these. Understanding and using your chakras can promote physical, emotional and spiritual healing, and can lend energy to your magickal work.

THE ROOT CHAKRA is located at the base of the spine. It is closest to the Earth, and can be utilized for Earthly grounding. It controls your physical vitality, 'flight or fight' response, physical survival instincts, and the emotions of desire, anger, jealousy and greed. Its color is red, *other colors associated with the Root Chakra are **black, brown**, and **gray**. Gemstones like hematite, bloodstone, black tourmaline, labodorite, garnet, ruby, onyx, fire agate, smoky quartz, star ruby and red jasper are beneficial in balancing this chakra.* The First, or Root, Chakra governs life lessons involving the lessons of the material world, such as survival, and stores information involving family beliefs and loyalty, you ability to stand up for yourself, superstition, instincts, physical pain or pleasure, and touch. Your sense of self esteem, safety and security are also based here. *An imbalance in the First Chakra may be indicated by a loss of interest in the 'real world' and practical survival, obsessions and addictions, volatile emotions, selfishness, restlessness and a lack of energy. Among the essential oils and flower essences used to balance the Root Chakra are corn, clematis, rosemary, ylang-ylang, myrrh, frankincense, benzoin, patchouli and sandalwood.* Foods that fuel the First Chakra are Root vegetables like carrots, potatoes, parsnips, radishes, beets, onions, garlic, Protein-rich foods like eggs, meats, beans, tofu and soy products, and peanut butter, and Spices like horseradish, hot paprika, chives, cayenne, and pepper.

THE NAVEL CHAKRA Is located just below the navel, about 2-3 fingers. It is also known as the Sacral, or Second Chakra. In Martial Arts, it is called the "Hara". It represents your sexuality, creativity, self esteem, pleasures and frustrations. Its color is orange. *Orange Gemstones like carnelian, orange tourmaline, tangerine quartz, fire opal, citrine, moonstone, and orange zincite help to bring this chakra into balance.* The Second Chakra governs life lessons involving blaming and guilt, manifesting, money and prosperity, sex, power, control, and it is the base of you creativity and sense of morality. Information stored in the Second Chakra involves feelings of duality, personal magnetism, your patterns of control, your sociability, and emotions and feelings. An imbalance in the Second Chakra may be experienced as an eating disorder, drug or alcohol addiction, depression, and intimacy issues, including impotence and frigidity. *Among the essential oils and flower essences used to balance the Second Chakra are all citrus oils, such as neroli, melissa, and orange. Also rose, hibiscus, jasmine, Indian Paintbrush, and lady's slipper.* Foods that fuel the second Chakra include sweet and tropical fruits like melons, mangos, strawberries, passion fruit, oranges, coconut, etc. Also Honey and Nuts and seeds like almonds, walnuts, peanuts, sunflower seeds etc. and Spices such as cinnamon, vanilla, carob, sweet paprika, sesame seeds, and caraway seeds.

THE SOLAR PLEXUS CHAKRA Is just above your navel, at the center of your solar plexus. Emotional memories are stored here, and it's where your 'gut feelings' come from. It is the seat of your emotional life, and many of us are naturally connected to our environments through this chakra. Its color is yellow. Gemstones like citrine, golden topaz, amber, yellow tourmaline and yellow sapphire are used to bring this chakra into balance. The Solar Plexus, or Third Chakra, governs life lessons involving your self esteem, a fear of rejection or an oversensitivity to criticism, distorted self-image, and a fear of your "secrets being found out". Information stored in the Third Chakra involves your personal power, your personality, your sense of 'knowing' and your sense of belonging. An imbalance in the Third Chakra may manifest as a difficulty concentrating, a poor ability to make decisions, or to judge a situation accurately, a feeling that you are more important, or less than, than other people and trouble taking action or getting things done. *Among the essential oils and flower essences used to balance the Third Chakra are yarrow, chamomile, peppermint, lemon juniper, vetivert, petigrain and marjoram.* Foods that fuel the Third Chakra are granola, grains, pastas, breads, cereal, rice, flax seed, sunflower seeds, etc. Dairy foods like milk, cheese, and yogurt, and spices like ginger, mints, melissa, chamomile, turmeric, cumin, and fennel.

THE HEART CHAKRA is in the heart. It is the center for unconditional love, tolerance, empathy, forgiveness, and compassion. It is the seat of the soul. Its color is green and the secondary color is pink. Gemstones like rose or green quartz, ruby zoisite, watermelon, pink or green tourmaline, aventurine, malachite, jade, emeralds, moss agate, peridot, and pink saphire are useful for bringing this chakra into harmony. The Heart, or Fourth Chakra, governs life lessons involving love and compassion, self confidence and self acceptance, inspiration and hope, generosity, and on the flip side, feelings of despair, hate, envy, fear, jealousy, and anger. Information stored in the Heart Chakra includes the connections or "heart strings" to those we love. An imbalance in the Heart Chakra may be felt as a lack of self discipline, difficulty in relationships, attempts to live vicariously through others, and depending on someone else for your happiness. *Among the essential oils and flower essences used to balance the Fourth Chakra are holly, poppy, rose, eucalyptus and pine, bergamot, melissa, jasmine or rosewood.* Foods that fuel the Heart Chakra are leafy greens and vegetables like spinach, kale, dandelion greens, broccoli, cauliflower, cabbage, celery, squash, etc. liquids like green and herbal teas, and spices such as basil, sage, thyme, cilantro, and parsley.

THE THROAT CHAKRA Is located in the throat, near the thyroid gland. It is the chakra of communication, expression and judgment. Its color is aqua or turquoise, secondary colors are various shades of light blue. Gemstones like turquoise, blue opal, blue topaz, fluorite, or blue lace agate balance this chakra. The Throat, or Fifth Chakra, governs life lessons of self expression and speaking one's truth, creativity (especially writing or speaking) faith, and making decisions and will power. On the flip side, issues of addiction, the need to criticize, lack of authority, and indecisiveness. Information stored in the Fifth Chakra includes self-knowledge and truth, attitudes, and the senses of hearing, taste, and smell. An imbalance in the Throat Chakra can be felt as difficulty in self expression, poor learning ability, habitual lying, fear, doubt, and uncertainty. *Among the essential oils and flower essences used to balance the Fifth Chakra are cosmos, trumpet vine, larch, blue chamomile, sage, lemongrass, geranium or hyssop.* Foods that fuel the Fifth Chakra are liquids in general, such as water, fruit juices, and herbal teas, tart or tangy fruits like lemons, limes, grapefruit, and kiwi, other tree growing fruits like apples, pears, plums, peaches, apricots, etc. and spices like salt, and lemon grass.

THE BROW CHAKRA is located in the center of the brain *(not the center of the forehead)*, and is also known as "the Third Eye". This chakra governs spiritual direction and wisdom. It is the seat of dreams, inner vision, and the spiritual life. Its color is indigo or shades of dark blue. Gemstones like lapis lazuli, purple flourite, sugalite, azurite or sodalite compliment this Chakra. Life lessons centering around the Brow Chakra include understanding, "reality checks", detachment, open mindedness, trusting your intuition and insights, and developing your psychic abilities. Self-realization, and releasing hidden and repressed negative thinking. The information stored within the Third Eye Chakra include seeing things clearly (symbolically or literally), wisdom, intuition, and intellect. An imbalance in the Sixth Chakra might be felt as a learning disability, co-ordination problems, or sleep disorders. *Among the essential oils and flower essences used to balance the Sixth Chakra are wild oat, Queen Anne's Lace, madia, rosemary, lavender, peppermint, spruce, frankincense, patchouli, elemi or clary sage.* Foods that fuel the Brow Chakra include dark bluish colored fruits such as blueberries, red and concord grapes, black berries, raspberries, etc. and liquids such as red wines and grape juice, and spices like lavender, poppy seed, and mugwort.

THE CROWN CHAKRA is located at the crown of the head. It balances the inner and outer person, and is the connection for the higher self. It is the channel through which we receive divine guidance, purpose and wisdom. Its color is purple, the secondary color is clear or white.

Gemstones like amethyst, clear quartz, diamonds, moldavite, and peacock ore are perfect for bringing the crown charka into alignment and balance. Life lessons to be learned through the Crown Chakra are intuitive knowing, integration of the whole Self, spirituality, living in the now, discovery of the Divine, the ability to see the big picture in the stream of Life, devotion, inspiration, values, ethics, trust, selflessness, humanitarianism. The information stored in the Seventh Chakra includes your connection to the Divine, your life's purpose, your connection to past lives, and Immortality. An imbalance in the Crown Chakra may be felt as lack of purpose, loss of meaning or identity, mental illness, and senility. *Among the essential oils and flower essences used to balance the Seventh Chakra are lotus, angelica, star tulip, frankincense, sandalwood, myrrh, jasmine, benzoin, neroli, lavender, angelica or St. John's Wort.* Foods that fuel the Seventh Chakra are... none! Fasting and detoxing are recommended, and using incense and smudging with herbs like sage, copal, myrrh, frankincense, and juniper.

Magickal Balance

The top three chakras- the crown, third eye and throat- are the seat of your masculine energy. They are responsible for critical and analytical thought, logic and reason.

The lower three chakras- the root, navel and solar plexus- are the seat of your feminine energy. They are responsible for your emotional reactions and memories, your creativity, and your capacity for childlike wonder and delight.

The heart chakra is where the male and female energies meet- it is the most potent place from which to imagine and visualize your desires. Staying centered in the heart will help you avoid the pointless mind chatter of the masculine, and the anxious worry of the feminine; stay focused on your heart's desire for the best magickal results! Controlling the flow of your own energy is not only the key to success in magick, but to your happiness, health and success in life. How do you do this? Through practicing the art of meditation.

ZHANG FU THEORY, CHAKRAS AND "CELLULAR MEMORY"

Have you ever considered the idea that you might not be storing all of your memories *in your head?* Many people believe that we also store our memories *in our bodies, especially the emotionally charged memories,* and that this can contribute, or even cause, physical illness and disease.

Have you ever considered that maybe, some of your persistent health complaints might be related to some of your other life difficulties? Or visa versa? Basically, the idea is, when we hold on to negative emotions, these are based in certain parts of the body, and will eventually manifest as a dis-ease. Also, there are certain theories about what organs go with what types of thoughts and emotions.

In traditional Chinese medicine, there is something known as "Zhang Fu theory". The theory states there are five Zhang (solid) organs and five Fu (hollow) organs. Each Zhang organ has a function, an element, an associated Fu organ, an associated emotion, spirit, etc.

ZHANG-FU RELATIONSHIPS, EMOTIONS, SPIRITS AND SPIRIT ACUPRESSURE POINTS

Element	Fire	Earth	Metal/Air	Water	Wood
Zhang Organ	heart	spleen	lungs	kidneys	liver
Related Fu Organ	Small intestine	stomach	Large intestine	bladder	gall bladder
Emotion	Joy	Pensiveness	Grief	Fear	Anger
Spirit	Cosmic Soul	Intellect	Corporeal Soul	Will	Ethereal Soul
Acupressure or Acupuncture point	*Shentang*-Spirit Hall-BL44 **Location:** ½ way between your armpit and spine on the left side of your back	*Yishe*-Idea Abode-BL49 **Location:** ½ way between your waist and spine on the left side of your back	*Pohu*-BL42 **Location:** ½ way between your shoulder/upper arm and spine on the left side of your back	*Zhishi*-Will Chamber-BL52 **Location:** 2" out from 2nd lumbar vertebrae, right above butt muscle on left side	*Hunmen*-Soul Gate-BL47 **Location:** 2" out from 9th thoracic vertebrae, middle back on left side

(Maybe next time you get a massage, try pressing these points, to see if anything emotional or mental can be released!)

THE SEVEN CHAKRAS * RELATED ORGANS AND ILLNESSES

The First Chakra:

Related organs- The spinal column, bones, feet, and the immune system.

Energy- physical safety, security, your ability to provide for life's necessities, courage and inner strength.

Physical disorders- Lower back pain, sciatica, varicose veins, rectal problems, depression, immune disorders.

Second Chakra:

Related organs- Sexual organs, large intestine, pelvis, appendix, bladder, hips.
Energy- Blame, guilt, money, sex, power and control, creativity, joy, sociability.
Physical disorders- Lower back pain, reproductive problems, urinary problems, constipation and/or diarrhea, gas and bloating.

Third Chakra:

Related organs- Abdomen, small intestine, liver, gallbladder, kidney and pancreas, adrenal glands, spleen.
Energy- Issues of trust, feelings of fear and intimidation, self-esteem, self-respect, caring for ones self and others, decisions, sensitivity to criticism, sense of honor.
Physical disorders- Arthritis, ulcers, diabetes, indigestion, eating disorders, liver.

Fourth Chakra:

Related organs- Heart and circulatory system, lungs, shoulders and arms, ribs, breasts, diaphragm, thymus gland.
Energy- Love and hate, resentment, bitterness, grief, anger, self-centeredness, loneliness, commitment, forgiveness, compassion, hope and trust.
Physical disorders- Heart disease, asthma, allergies, bronchial conditions, upper back, shoulder, breast cancers.

Fifth Chakra:

Related organs- Throat, thyroid, mouth, teeth, gums, esophagus.
Energy- Sense of choice and personal expression, strength of will, following your dream, using your personal power to create, addictions, judgment, criticism, faith and knowledge, ability to make decisions.
Physical disorders- sore throat, raspy voice, mouth ulcers, gum disease, TMJ, swollen glands, thyroid problems.

Sixth Chakra:

Related organs- The brain, nervous system, eyes, ears, nose, pineal gland, and pituitary gland.

Energy- Self evaluation, truth, intellect, sense of adequacy, openness to new ideas, your ability to learn from experience, emotional intelligence, connection to intuition.

Physical disorders- Brain disorders, neurological disorders, blindness, deafness, learning disabilities, seizures.

Seventh Chakra:

Related organs- Muscular system, skeletal system, skin.

Energy- Ability to trust in the process of life, personal values, ethics, courage, humanitarianism, faith, inspiration, spirituality and devotion.

Physical Disorders- Energetic disorders, depression, chronic fatigue, extreme sensitivity to light or sound.

OK, so where am I going with this? Just demonstrating that this is an old and valid theory, and to maybe give you some food for thought. What are your predominant, negative emotions? Where do your health problems manifest? And might any of this relate in any way to the reasons why you have problems making or keeping money? With why you feel you don't have enough? Relationship problems? Can the feelings in your body give any clues to what is going on in your subconscious? And can working with this not only help your physical and emotional health, but also your relationships and financial health?

Hawaiian Shamans believe that memory is held in the muscles; have you ever just blanked out, and forgotten someone's name? Maybe the muscle where that name was stored was tensed! This theory may explain why hypnosis can sometimes uncover hidden memories- when the muscles are completely relaxed in a hypnotic trance, the memories are more easily accessed.

With all this in mind, consider our next topic....

MEDITATION

Meditation is important to the practice of magick- it will help you to gain control of your mind and your energy field, the only 'magickal tools' you will ever really need! It can also help you to heal your body, mind and emotions. Here are three easy meditations you can try.

Five Pointed Star Meditation

Find a quiet place and time, where you can have at least fifteen minutes of peace and quiet. Lie down, with your arms and legs gently spread apart- comfortably, and not too wide. Make sure your hands are facing palms up.

Feel yourself sinking into the floor, just melting and glowing, feeling very heavy. Locate the minor chakras in your hands and feet- your hand chakras are in the center of your palms, and your feet chakras are in the center of the arch of each foot. Open these chakras up, and feel energy flowing through them, up your arms and legs. Let the energy flow up to your heart chakra- combine the energy from your arms and legs in your heart center. From the heart center, let the energy flow freely upwards, through the center of your head, and out the crown chakra. Let this energy fountain out through your crown, flowing out into your aura. Feel your aura glowing big and bright, like a star.

Keep 'glowing' until you feel your energy field is whole and complete. Gently relax the flow of energy, until you feel solid, and back in the 'real world'. Your mind should now be free of clutter, and your body should feel both energized and relaxed!

☆

Sacred Tree Meditation

The Buddha found Enlightenment while meditating under a Bo tree. This quick and easy meditation may not free you from the Cycles of Rebirth or the Wheel of Karma, but it might just free you from the psychic stress and tensions of your day to day life, thus enabling you to focus more clearly on your true purpose, magickal or otherwise.

Find a quiet place and time, take off your shoes, close your eyes, and stand with your hands hanging heavily at your side. Imagine yourself surrounded by a warm, white light, and breathe this energy in, deeply and slowly.

Feel your feet on the floor, and imagine growing roots- let these roots grow way down deep, right to the center of the Earth. As these roots ground you and connect you to our Mother Earth; release all the psychic negativity of your day- release all the people, the problems, all the responsibilities back to the Earth. Breathe deeply, and feel all the energy that's been keeping you from feeling grounded and centered drain out, and into the core of the Earth.

Now, imagine your roots absorbing the nourishment Mother Earth has to offer- feel this warm, powerful energy from the Earth's core rise up through your roots, through your feet, your legs, your hips, your torso. When you feel the energy reach your head, let your tree grow "branches". Reach these branches up into the Universe, far out into the Cosmos. Feel the psychic energy of the Universe flowing through your "branches", through your head, and down through your trunk. Allow this Cosmic energy to flow right down through your roots, into the Earth. Feel the Earth energy rising up, the Cosmic flowing down. You are now grounded to the Earth, and in tune with the Cosmos.

When you are ready, call back all the psychic energy you've lost and left behind through out the day, and gather it up into a hot, glowing golden sun above your head. Let this golden sun of your own psychic energy envelope you, flowing through your head, down your arms, filling up your entire body, right down to your feet. If you want, make another gold sun to shine down and nourish your 'tree'. When you are ready, open your eyes, stretch, and feel refreshed!

A More Advanced Meditation

This is a more advanced meditation technique, which builds on what you have learned from the five Pointed Star and Sacred Tree mediations. It is broken down into five lessons- master each lesson before moving onto the next. This meditation technique is very powerful, and has nothing to do with the common notion that meditation is about "sitting around cross legged, not thinking about anything". It will engage the energies of your own body and aura for a powerful spiritual cleansing, thus clearing the way for personal growth and healing on all levels. If you like, you can read this section into a tape recorder, to create your own meditation tape!

Lesson One – Grounding

Get comfortable sitting in a chair, feet on the floor, close your eyes, and relax. Now, bring your attention to you body, noticing how it feels; Is there any tightness, gripping, numbness, pain or agitation anywhere in your body?

Take a deep breath, and notice the base of your spine, which is your 1st chakra. The 1st chakra is where you will create a "grounding cord". When you make a grounded connection to the Earth, it stabilizes your body, and allows you to release pent up energy back to the planet.

Mentally, see and feel a bright spot of energy at your 1st chakra. Notice what happens to your body when you say hello to your 1st chakra, notice how it feels.

Next, notice the planet- send a hello deep down into the center of the Earth. Notice how your body feels to acknowledge the center of the planet.

Next, you will create a grounding cord - imagine a picture you'd like to use; it could be a beam of light, a waterfall, a tree, an umbilical cord, a rope. Feel the bright spot of energy at the base of your spine, and send another hello to the center of the planet. Now, step back mentally, and connect your 1st chakra with the center of the planet using your image. Send your grounding cord deep down into the center of the planet. Notice what happens to your body when you connect the two points - does your body release energy? Do you feel yourself coming back, deeper into yourself? Do you feel more solid? More relaxed?

Take a deep breath, and consciously decide to release energy - just let go of your day, your job, your responsibilities, at least for now, and allow yourself to connect with your body. Release any pent up energy, any pain, stiffness, tension or blockages from anywhere in your body down through your grounding cord. How does it feel to release energy? Notice your body, and use your grounding cord to release and relax. Notice if you're tight or tense anywhere- these are points where you may be carrying foreign energy- we can pick up energy from other people, from places and situations, and store it in our bodies. Say hello to them, and let go- don't force or push the energy out, just let it drop out. Release all the foreign energy point by point, letting it fall through your body and down your grounding cord, back to the center of the Earth.

When all of the negative energies are released, and you feel very relaxed, you'll need to replenish your energy- but you don't want to replace it with the same energy you just released!. Instead, imagine a golden sun above your head, and call back your own energy from where ever you left it- at work, with other people, wherever. Make your sun big and bright, and let it flow through the top of your head and into all the places you've released. Let it flow through your entire body, filling up your feet, your hands, your fingers. If you want, make another sun.

When you're full, take a deep breath, open your eyes, stretch, and enjoy the feeling of being grounded.

Lesson Two - Creating Space

Get comfortable in your chair, take a deep breath, and say hello to your body. How do you feel? Settle in, close your eyes, and notice your entire body, especially your skin. Notice your size- how does it feel?

Notice your 1st chakra and the center of the planet, and send a hello to the two points. Create a grounding cord and connect. How does your body feel to connect and release energy?

Bring your awareness to your body again. Notice your "space"- your space is your aura. Become aware of this energy around you, feel its size, imagine a bubble of energy under your feet, over your head, behind you, in front of you. What happens to your body when you notice this space, your aura? How do you feel?

Continue to stay aware of your grounding cord. You can carry negative and foreign energy in your aura, too. Release any negative and foreign energy from your aura, (you don't need to identify it) just release it, and let it go.

Take a deep breathe. Now, notice your room - take your aura, and extend it to fill up the room. How does that feel? Sometimes your aura is big, sometimes it's small- do you feel you lose a sense of yourself, if you extend it too big? Now, extend it to encompass the building- how does that feel? Are you comfortable doing this? If it feels uncomfortable, try it anyway, just for the experience.

Now bring your aura back to the room, then back to your body, about two feet around your body. Next, pull it in another foot, then pull it in to six inches. How does that feel? Do you feel like you don't have enough space? Now bring it back to about two feet. Find a comfortable place. Sometimes just moving your aura around shakes out the alien and negative energy.

Notice your grounding cord, and continue to release energy. Now, get the idea of "owning" your space- in the owning and creating of space for yourself, you set the stage to heal yourself, as a spirit. Once you feel that ownership, create a golden sun, and bring your energy back from where you left it. Make the sun at least as big as your space, or even bigger. Bring the sun in, fill up your body and your aura. When you are ready, open your eyes, stretch, and enjoy the feeling of owning your space.

Lesson Three - The center of your head

Get comfortable, take a deep breath, notice your surroundings, notice your body, and relax. Notice the base of your spine and send a hello to the center of the planet. Connect the two with a line of energy, creating a grounding cord.

Once you are grounded, take a deep breath, and notice where your attention is. Is it on your body, your spouse, on your job, on your kids? As you get an idea of where your attention is, get the idea of bringing it back to yourself, back to your body.

As an experiment, become aware of your right hand. Put your attention in the palm of your hand. Notice what it feels like to have your attention in the palm of your hand. Next, notice your left foot, *be* in your left foot. Notice your nose -let yourself *be* at the tip of your nose. Then notice your eyes- move back until your attention is right behind your eyes- how does it feel to be in the center of your head? Notice what you find there- is it noisy? Are there thoughts there, or other people? Notice what is there, then notice that *you* are not any of these things, - *you* are the *awareness* in the center of your head.

Now, take a deep breathe, and release whatever it is you've found in the center of your head. Release it down your grounding cord, just let go of those thoughts, images and sensations. What happens when you let go? Notice how much room there is in the center of your head- as you let go, does that give *you* more room?

Now decide how you can create the center of your head as a sanctuary for yourself. You can create a beautiful room, or a landscape, a color, a feeling of warmth. Create it just for yourself. Is it big enough? Notice what happens to your body when you settle into the center of your head. Acknowledge your body, and yourself in the center of your head.

Next, create a golden sun, and let it flow through the center of your head. Make another sun, and let it flow through and fill up the rest of your body. When you are all full, open your eyes, stretch, and enjoy the new perspective from the center of your head.

Lesson Four – Separation

Relax, take a deep breath, and say hello to your 1st chakra. Send a hello into the center of the planet, and create a grounding cord.

Put your awareness into the center of your head. Imagine a big golden sun, and call back all your energy into that golden sun. Once you've collected up all your energy, allow the golden sun to flow through the top of your head, through the center of your head, and fill up your entire body. Do you feel a change once you're grounded and filled with your own energy?

Now, about eight inches from your forehead, get an image of your favorite flower, or maybe a bubble, or a miniature sun. Can you sense it? Can you feel it? Now release this image, and create another one- it could be another flower, or bubble or sun, or you could experiment with something different. Now release this image, just let it go, let it float away.

Notice the center of your head, notice the space around you, find the edge of your space, your aura. Notice you can also use your grounding cord to ground your aura.

Now, in front of you, get another image of a flower, or bubble or sun, but this time, with the idea that this image represents you, on an energy level. What does this image look like? Is it vibrant or dull? Solid or wilted? If you don't like it, release it and make another- just do this until you get something you like.

Now set your image on the edge of your aura. Allow it to be between you and all the energies around you. Allow it to provide some separation between the demands and expectations the world has of you. Get a sense of your job- let it be between you and your job. Get a sense of a person you work with- let your image be between you and this person, giving you space. You can even use it to give yourself space from your family.

As you find your separation from the things around you, you create more space for yourself. This space gives you the freedom to be you, to enjoy your own energy and ideas. Think of something you are supposed to be doing, a task, and allow yourself some space from it. How does that feel?

Allow your image to remain at the edge of your aura. Once you've found a sense of separation, create a golden sun, and fill yourself up. As you fill up, get a sense of owning your space, and owning your ability to be separate from the energies, expectations, people and things around you.

Lesson Five - Running Energy

Settle in, take a deep breath, and relax into your body. Notice the base of your spine, and send a hello to your 1st chakra. Notice the center of the planet, and send a hello to it. Then create a grounding cord, and connect these two points with a grounding cord.

Now bring your attention behind your eyes, into the center of your head. Notice your space, notice your body, notice your grounding.

Create your favorite separation image, and set it out in front of you, right at the edge of your aura. This allows you to separate from the energy around you, and go within.

Take a deep breath, and be aware of yourself in the center of your head. Then notice your feet. Right in the arch of each foot are your feet chakras. Say hello to your feet chakras, and allow them to open up.

Now, send a hello into the center of the planet, and look deep within the planet for some Earth energy. It might be a color, an image, a vast underground lake, or a great, glowing underground pool of lava.

Bring that Earth energy up, like a line of energy, coming up through the planet. Allow your feet chakras to draw this energy up, let it flow through your legs, and imagine the Earth energy flowing up through your legs to the 1st chakra. When the energy reaches the 1st chakra, allow it to fall back down your grounding cord. Notice what happens to your body when you run Earth energy.

Take a deep breath, notice yourself in the center of your head, and notice that the Earth energy keeps on flowing- once it starts, it automatically keeps flowing, like a siphon.

Next, notice the top of your head, your crown chakra. Say hello to your crown chakra, and imagine opening it up. Send a hello out to the Universe, go way out, past the atmosphere, past the planet, beyond the Solar System, way out into space. Now, find an energy you'd like to bring in. Start to call that energy down to the top of your head, right into the back part of your crown chakra. Allow that energy to flow down your back channels, on either side of your spine, into the 1st chakra.

Allow the Earth energy and the Cosmic energy to mix within the 1st chakra, and then let it flow back up through the front channels. As it flows through your body, it cleans out and energizes all your chakras.

When it reaches your 5th chakra at your throat, allow some energy to flow down your arms, and out through your fingers.

The rest of the energy will flow up through your crown chakra, and fountain out of your head, into your aura.

Take a deep breath, be aware of yourself in the center of your head, and notice what it feels like to run energy.

Allow the energy to flow as long as you like. When you are ready, create a golden sun of your own energy above your head. Call back all your energy, and collect it up into a bright, hot golden sun. Then let it flow through your head, filling up your entire body.

As you master the technique, try running different colors of Cosmic energy through your aura. You can use the colors related to the chakras, or any other color that comes to mind. See how running blue, green, yellow, pink, red, violet or blue makes your feel. If a particular color makes you feel good, go ahead and run it!

Lesson Six – Creating

Use all the meditation tools you have learned up til now, and get grounded, create some space, get into the center of your head, find some separation, and begin running your energy.

This next technique will be similar to the separation technique; in front of you, get an image of a flower, or bubble or sun, or whatever image you like to use, and explode it. Make another one, and explode that one too. Now make another one, and use that one for your creation.

Start to get an idea of what you want to create. Imagine it, feel it, and love it. Get a picture of it. Put that picture into your flower, bubble, or sun, and put as much detail into it as you can, think or and imagine every little detail you can. Just imagine it going right into your image. Now, see yourself in the creation; see yourself having it, put yourself right in there with it, having.

Next, ground this image, create a grounding cord to make it more solid. And as you ground it, if there is any energy in it that is not yours, any energy that says you can't have it, alters it, or makes it difficult to see it clearly, ground it out, just let it drain out of the picture, and let the whole creation get brighter.

Now, take this picture, and bring it into your aura. Notice how you feel, how your body feels, when experience this creation. Move it back out of your aura, and experience having it, and owning it. It is yours.

Next, call all of your *own energy* back from this image, bring it back to yourself. When this is done, release it into the Universe, just let it go, and float away to the center of the Cosmos.

Create another flower, bubble or sun in front of you, and gather up all the energy that might prevent you from having your creation, anything that says it is not possible, you are not good enough, etc, and release it into your image. When this is done, explode it, blow it up, to relase and neutralize that energy.

Create a golden sun over your head, and create lots of energy for you to have your creation into this sun. Bring that golden sun into the top of your head, filling your entire body and aura.

So that's it. Practice releasing the trapped, negative energy from your body, and running pure, clean energy from our Mother Earth and the Cosmos. Practice giving yourself "space", and refresh yourself with *your own* golden sun energy. You may be surprised with the cleansing effect these exercises have on your body, and you may also be surprised with what gets released! You may experience emotions, thoughts, remember events or people.... Let them go! And create! Releasing the blockages will allow your energy to flow more freely, healing your body, mind, spirit, and hopefully your outer life circumstances, including your ability to create magick!

As you master the technique, try running different colors of Cosmic energy through your aura. See how running blue, green, yellow, pink, red, violet or blue makes your feel. If a particular color makes you feel good, go ahead and run it!

So that's it. See, meditation isn't that hard, and with just a little practice and a few minutes a day, it can make all the difference in how you feel, and more importantly, how you feel about life.

REIKI

Since we have been on the subject of energy, healing, and meditation, I will also include a section on using and activating Reiki Symbols.

THE JAPANESE SYMBOL FOR REIKI

In Master level Reiki, you have access to the Sacred Reiki Symbols. These are handed down from Master to Master, and are used for attuning others into the Reiki Energy, and more importantly, they can be used for healing and protection. In this very special section, I will pass these symbols along to you.

The Reiki symbols are a means of focusing your attention, in order to connect with the particular healing frequencies symbolized by these signs.

On the following pages are the five Reiki symbols I now pass on to you!

CHU KU RAY

Pronounced "choh-koo-ray"

"The Power Symbol"

"God and Man Coming Together" or "I have the key"

The principal use of this symbol is to increase Reiki power. It draws Energy from around you, and it focuses it where you want to.

Make the sign over your heart, and say the words Cho Ku Rei 3 times, while imagining pictures of yourself with increased wealth, or whatever else you desire.

It is an all-purpose symbol. It can be used for anything, anywhere, anytime, such as to cleanse negative energies, for spiritual protection, to bless food, water, medicine, herbs, *to aid in manifestation,* to seal energies after you do the other exercises in this book, and to empower other Reiki Symbols

Hint- If you wish to use the symbol to bring Energy to yourself, reverse it. Use it as drawn to help other people.

SEI HEI KI

Pronounced "say-hay-key"

The Mental/Emotional Symbol

"God and Man Coming Together" or "The Key to the Universe"

This symbol is used primary for mental and emotional healing, and for calming the mind. It is very useful for psychic protection and cleansing, to activate the Ki energy, to balance the right and left brain. This symbol also aids in removing addictions, healing past traumas clearing emotional blockages and removing negative energies and bad vibrations (including the mental addictions, past traumas, blockages and negative energies that keep you poor!)

This symbol restores emotional balance and harmony. Trace it over your abdomen while saying the words SEI HEI KI (pronounced "say-hay-key") slowly and deliberately three times. You can also trace this symbol and place it under your pillow while you sleep, to encourage peaceful sleep, and wonderful dreams of health, wealth and love!

HON SHA ZE SHO NEN

Pronunciation: Hanh-shah-zay-show-nen

The Distance Symbol

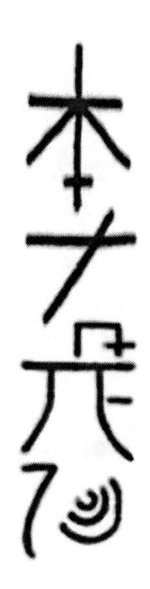

**"The God in Me Greets the God in You,
to Promote Enlightenment and Peace"**

This is the distance healing symbol, and it is used to send Reiki over distance and time (past, present, and future), to anyone at anytime.

If you wish to use this to help another person, place your hand over it, close your eyes, and imagine sending healing energy and love to that person- yes, it's that easy to send out good vibrations to anyone and everyone!

TAM-A-RA-SHA

Pronunciation: Tam-ara-sha

The Balancing Factor

This symbol is a balancing and unblocking symbol. It grounds and balances energy, helping to unblock the chakra energy centers along the spine, allowing the energy to flow ore freely and abundantly.

To use this symbol, try drawing the symbol with your finger over each of your chakras, especially the root, navel, heart and brow chakras. Or, you can visualize this symbol during meditation. Begin at the root chakra, and visualize this symbol rising up, clearing all your chakras as it goes!

It is also a nice talisman to carry with you in your wallet- simply draw it on a slip of paper, and keep it with your money!

DAI KO MYO

Pronounced "dye-ko-me-o"

The Master Symbol

This is the most powerful symbol in Reiki.
It can be used only by Reiki Masters.

This symbol is used to heal the soul; since it deals with the soul and our spiritual self, it heals disease, illness (and conditions such as poverty) *from the original source,* in the aura and energy field.

It helps to foster enlightenment and peace. It also works to clear blockages to becoming more intuitive- the better your intuition, the clearer your vision will be to finding your way to the peace, happiness and prosperity you seek! Like the Lightening it symbolizes, this symbol brings profound life changes on an energetic level.

METHODS FOR REIKI SYMBOL ACTIVATION

The symbols can be activated in any of the following ways:

By drawing them with your palm, while projecting energy outwards

By drawing them with your finger

By visualizing them

By spelling the symbol's name three times.

By saying the symbol's name three times.

*You can use whatever method you wish, but don't forget that it's the **intent** that counts.*

To help your friends and family with Reiki symbols-

First place the symbol in the palm of your own hand, and then redraw or visualize the same symbol on the other person's crown chakra, the palm of that person's hand, or if they are sick or in pain, the areas to be treated (of course, please recognize, that doing this does not replace proper medical treatment for serious illness!)

With practice, the actual symbols will become less relevant, and your focus will change to the *intent* of the specific symbols.

PSYCHIC PROTECTION

Developing your ability to protect yourself on a psychic level is at least as important as developing your psychic ability to "predict the future"; in fact, it's more important. We are immersed in a sea of psychic energy, and as members of our individual families, social groups, and society at large, we are constantly being pushed and pulled on energy levels we may not be aware of; most of this activity is unintentional, perhaps well meaning, but it will still lead you astray from who you are, and your true purpose. The energy you may be projecting towards others, with the intention of influence, is also something you need to protect *yourself* from; it may seem you only have good intentions, but in the long run, you will be doing yourself more harm than good if you try to accomplish your goals by *reaching out* with your energy or aura. This is a basic violation of 'good boundaries', and if you take it too far, it will lapse into the realm of 'psychic vampirism'.

So what can you do about it? First, use the techniques you've learned through the meditation exercises to keep yourself grounded and centered; the optimum center is to stay between your heart chakra and your third eye, but you must allow your energy to run where it will when it needs to. Just don't 'dwell' in your stomach, and also, stay away from your forehead; the 'third eye' *is not* in the center of your forehead, but back about two inches, in the center of your *brain*. Dwelling between your eyes at the center of your *forehead* stimulates 'mind chatter', and even paranoia; pulling your attention back to the center of your brain stimulates *'perception'*. Sounds crazy, but give it a try- pull your attention back, and see how it calms your thoughts.

Keeping yourself grounded is also important; you can use the grounding cord technique learned in the advanced meditation throughout your day, but that might be difficult if you are under stress- if so, try the following technique. Feel your feet 'glowing'- this will simultaneously ground you, and also run just enough Earth Energy to keep you feeling calm and centered. It's very easy, but effective.

If you are in a situation where someone is projecting energy with the intent to control you (like at your job, or maybe your family) running the color blue through your aura can be an effective protection technique. Also, remember to keep the 'separation image' you learned to use in the Advanced Meditation at the edge of your aura. Use it to absorb 'foreign' energy, and periodically either let the image float away, or explode it, then create a new one. If the attention being thrown your way is very intense and negative, try putting up an imaginary mirror to reflect it back! You may be surprised at how quickly this attention stops! *But no matter what you do, do not send any of your own attention or energy back.* You may be obliged to listen and interact with the person, but don't 'reach out' with your own energy; stay nice and secure, bathed in the familiar warmth your own aura. As soon as you get a chance, use one of the meditation techniques to help cleanse your aura of negativity, and rebalance your energy. Learning to define your own boundaries on an energy level, and also learning to respect the boundaries of others, might just be the freedom you've been looking for!

Beings Without Bodies

Psychic protection does not only encompass protection from people; there are "Beings without bodies" all around, and at times, these "Beings" can attach to your aura.

These Beings generally fall into two categories: those who were once incarnated as people, and those who weren't. Those who were once incarnated as people are "ghosts", and those who weren't go by many names, and can be good or not so good... and almost invariably, it is those who are not so good who are drawn to attach to a living being's aura. They do this to draw energy, to live life through that person, or to use that person's body and mind for their own purposes.

The idea of "channeling" a Higher Being may seem romantic, or some might be drawn to the notion of controlling "Familiars" to do their bidding, but unless you have had serious training, *don't try it*. This may not be what you want to hear, but there are many negative entities who are just waiting to be "invited in", and they are quite capable of masquerading as a Higher Being, an Ascended Master, a god or goddess, or a dearly departed relative. And once you let them in, they can be very, very hard to get rid of. And they can really mess up your life, *big time*.

To protect yourself from such Beings, use the techniques outlined in the Advance Meditation. Keep yourself grounded, and ground out any negative energy you might feel in your body. Often, you may feel a spiritual "attachment" physically. Let it go. And really learn to maintain the integrity of your aura. Feel it, fluff it up, and run energy through it. The stronger your aura is, the more it will be resistant to all attacks.

Most importantly, avoid indulging in negative emotions and bad habits; negative entities feed on negative emotions, and encourage bad habits. They will amplify negative thoughts, maybe drive you to drink or do drugs, cause friction and fights with friends and family, in order to stimulate more negative emotions to feed on. What's bad for you is great for a negative entity! Don't give them much to work with, and more importantly, if you foster goodness in yourself and your life, you are less likely to attract them in the first place. Learn to readily let go of fear, anger, judgment, lust, vengeance, self pity, whatever dark emotions you harbor, and you are well on your way to both emotional and spiritual freedom.

There are many good books on the subject of psychic self defense, and also on spirit "possession". Please make it a subject of self interest, and read at least a few books on these subjects. Make a habit of practicing the techniques that work for you; this is something that must be practiced if you are to seriously advance in your spiritual growth and magickal abilities.

BREATHING

Most of us haven't learned to breathe; shallow breathing can cause problems on many levels. When we are constantly 'holding our breathe', carbon dioxide will build up in the blood stream, causing unnecessary anxiety, and clouded thinking.

Breathing deeply and slowly, as if in sleep, is the optimum way to breathe during meditation, and at times when you need to contemplate or calm yourself. Relax your diaphragm, and draw your breathe all the way down into your belly. Pause, then fully exhale, feeling your warm breathe as it passes through the center of your body, up into your 'Third Eye', and out your nose.

This next technique is a good one to try to remember all the time; imagine breathing in a purifying White Light energy, and thoroughly exhaling all your negativity as a smoke. You will be absolutely amazed!

Breathing into your chakras is a technique worth learning and using. Breathing all the way down to the navel chakra in your belly, and breathing out through your crown chakra at the top of your head will produce a sense of euphoria during meditation, though it may be too disorienting to do while out in the 'real world'. Breathing into your heart chakra, and exhaling through your brow chakra is a good basic technique to use in your everyday dealings with the 'real world'. Oddly, you may notice that while using this technique, your sense of smell becomes more acute- that's just one more 'sensory clue' you can learn to use. You may notice that certain people have certain distinctive, common odors, which you may learn to recognize as chronic fear, sexual preoccupation, or drug or alcohol abuse.

Some of these ideas and techniques concerning energy, meditation, chakras, auras and such may seem foreign to the way you have been taught to *think*. But that's the point- most of us have been encouraged to think, but not to *experience* ourselves (or others) as an energy, or even as a physical body. Our ability for critical thought is what separates us from the rest of the animal kingdom, for good and for worse. The psychic 'sixth sense' may be nothing more than the human animal's natural instincts, and an animal's instincts guide it to the environments that will allow it to flourish. Our 'critical' thinking can often be the biggest stumbling block on the magickal path; how much of what you think you want is really the influence of what society, your family, or your job expects of you? This energetic 'static' will interfere with following your instincts, and your instincts are your natural, magickal 'tool' for finding the environments that will allow *you* to truly flourish!

DREAMING

Shamans from every culture have relied on the interpretation of dreams for everything from curing illness, to predicting the future. Begin keeping a dream diary; a series of dreams is sometimes easier to interpret than a single dream, and often, our dreams are 'serialized'. The most important imagery will be repeated, and the basic theme behind the dreams will become more apparent.

The language of dreams is symbols and metaphors, and you will begin to understand your own personal associations with dream imagery the more you examine it. Also understand the cultural significance of your dream images- the Statue of Liberty, for instance, has a certain symbolism to the culture of the United States, but it also might have a personal significance to you, or to your own feelings about your culture. Also learn to draw parallels with the archetypal symbolism contained in folklore, history, fairytales, religion, and mythology with your dreams.

Dreams are not isolated, and cannot be separated from your everyday life. What is bothering you lately? What are you worried about? And how might the dream relate to that? Try this- meditate on a specific dream, allow the imagery to develop freely, without making a conscious effort to change it. Simply observes how the image gradually develops- this may lead you to the answer you are seeking.

You can also learn to request a dream as an answer to a certain problem, to aid in understanding the source of an illness, or to see your path in life more clearly.

If you are ill, or have pain anywhere in your body, try this; request to have a dream about the root cause of the problem, then gently and lovingly ask that part of your body to speak to you in your dreams. Focus a feeling of love and understanding, a willingness to listen, on that part of your body as you go to sleep. Keep your dream journal nearby, so you can record your dream! You may be very surprised at the results; often, suppressed feelings of revenge or regret, fear, longing and disappointment are at the root of the problem.

Common Dream Elements, and what they might mean-

Animals can represent your physical body, primal desires, and sexuality, depending on the qualities of the specific animal. Animals symbolize the untamed aspects of yourself.

To dream of fighting with an animal points to a hidden part of yourself that you are struggling to reject and push back into your subconscious. What animal is it, and what might it represent to you? Can you learn to love and accept it?

To dream of talking animals represents higher knowledge and wisdom. Listen to what this 'spirit animal' has to say; these dreams are very special! These are dreams that can guide you to reclaim the instincts and intuitions you have lost in your human incarnation.

To dream you are saving the life of an animal suggests a need to accept and value the emotions and characteristics represented by that animal, and that deep down, you do not wish to lose it. The dream may also mean you are feeling overwhelmed in day to day life; what is it that the animal represents, and how might that be threatened in yourself? How can you nurture and protect it?

To dream of lab animals denotes feeling dehumanized, and your true nature is repressed and devalued by those around you. You need to allow yourself to feel natural, despite the unnatural surroundings you may find yourself in!

Celebrities represent your pursuit of recognition as an individual. In our modern age, the movie stars, musicians, athletes and politicians we see in the media act as the 'archetypes' of our 'collective unconscious'- they exist both as real people in a mundane world, and they also exist as larger than life heroes and villains, gods and goddesses, victims, saints and tricksters, that exist on a plane that is both Universal and deeply personal. Who do you dream of, and what do they represent? What do they say or do in your dream? Do they give you advice or guidance? How are you like them, or how do you want to be like them? Use these questions to probe your own values, need for recognition and acceptance.

Angels can point to a troubled soul; perhaps you are worried about something, or maybe, you are deceiving yourself about what is in your own heart. Pay careful attention to the message angels bring. These messages can serve as a guide toward greater fulfillment and happiness, and they are often heralds of redemption, and of brighter times to come.

Demons represent ignorance, negativity, feelings of revenge, and your shadow self. They warn of overindulgence, lust, and poor choices made as the result of addictions. This is a warning to turn away from the darkness, towards the light. To ignore this message could put your physical and mental health in danger. To dream that you are possessed by demons indicates the ultimate inability to take responsibility for one's own actions.

Chase dreams may represent your way of coping with fear, stress or uncertain situations in your life. Instead of confronting the situation, you are running away and avoiding it. Examine the one chasing you, and you may gain some understanding and insight on the source of your fears. Your own feelings of anger, jealousy, and fear can sometimes manifest as a dream attacker. Next time you have a chase dream, turn around and confront your pursuer. Ask them why they are chasing you.

Flying dreams may mean you have gained a higher perspective on your life. The ability to control your flight represents your own personal sense of power. If you are flying with ease and joy, it suggests that you are on top of a situation, you have risen above it. Difficulties in flight indicates a lack of power in controlling your own circumstances. Things like power lines, trees, or mountains may block your flight. These barriers represent particular obstacles in your progress. You need to identify who or what is keeping you from moving forward.

If you fear flying, or feel you are flying too high, it suggests you are afraid of challenges, and afraid of success.

Falling dreams are an indication of insecurity, instability, and anxiety. You feel overwhelmed and out of control. This may reflect your relationships, or your work environment. Falling dreams often reflect a sense of failure or inferiority; it may be a fear of failure, loss of status, or loss in love.

Nakedness can symbolize a variety of things, depending on your situation. If the realization that you are walking around naked in public causes shame, it is often a reflection of your vulnerability. You may be feeling the need to hide something about yourself, and are afraid that others can see right through you. The dream might be telling you that you are trying to be something you are not. Finding yourself naked at work or in school suggests you are unprepared for a project. Many times, when you are naked in a dream, no one else seems to notice. This indicates your fears are unfounded; no one will notice your perceived faults or vulnerability except you. You may be magnifying the situation and making something out of nothing. Also, such dreams may indicate your desire (and failure) to get noticed.

Taking a test usually has to do with your sense of self esteem and confidence, or your lack of it. These dreams indicate a feeling of being put to the test or scrutinized in some way. These dreams also suggest you may feel unprepared for a challenge. Dreams of this nature also indicate that you are judging yourself by the standards of others. This may be a signal to examine an aspect of yourself that you may be neglecting.

Dream interpretation is a very personal and rewarding art- read as much as you can about it, and approach it with an open mind and heart. Learn to look objectively at the content of your own mind, as reflected in your dreams. To go with a 'cookbook' method of dream analysis will get you nowhere; you must learn to think for yourself, and understand the significance of your own iconography. The works of C.G. Jung, Joseph Campbell, and the sleeping prophet himself, Edgar Cayce will be valuable tools.

Remember, it's all about energy; you can learn a lot about metaphysics not only from Wiccan authors, but from studying the philosophies of

Hinduism, Buddhism, Kabala, Theosophy, the Native American and ancient Egyptian religions, as well as the works of many more great thinkers, who you are bound to encounter on your road to self discovery!

CORRESPONDENCES

PLANETARY

ELEMENTAL

GENDER

OILS HERBS AND STONES

BASIC CORRESPONDENCES

What are correspondences?

Let's say you are a Capricorn woman- you are ruled by the planet Saturn and the element of Earth, and your gender is female. These 'correspondences' influence your personality. Everything in nature is ruled by a certain planet, element, and has a certain gender- thus, it's 'personality'. This influences the type of spell work the ingredient is best suited for. Here is a list of basic correspondences- gender, elemental, planetary, days of the week and moon phases. You can use this information when choosing herbs, oils, incense and stones and the timing of your spell work.

GENDER

Masculine correspondence is strong and active. Use for protection, purification, hex-breaking, exorcism, lust, sexual potency, health, strength, courage, and financial success.

Feminine correspondence is subtler and softer. Use to attract love, increase beauty, youth, healing, develop psychic abilities, increase fertility, draw wealth, promote happiness and peace, aid sleep and cause visions.

ELEMENTAL

EARTH- A Feminine element
Direction- north
Color- green
Elemental beings- gnomes
Elemental animals- the bull, buffalo, stag, cows, ants, burrowing animals like gophers and prairie dogs, and the mouse
Stones- onyx, jade, amethyst, cat's eye, agate, calcite, fluorite

Metals- lead and iron

Earth rules spells and rituals dealing with fertility, jobs, money, business, health, ecology and nature, and stability.

AIR- A Masculine element
Direction- east
Color- yellow
Elemental beings- sylphs
Elemental animals- birds, winged insects, spiders, the fox, wolf, raccoons, and turtles
Stones- moonstone, mica, turquoise, aventurine, and jasper
Metals- aluminum, tin and mercury

Air rules spells and rituals dealing with memory and intellect, test taking, divination and psychic ability, travel, and overcoming addictions.

FIRE- A Masculine element
Direction- south
Color- red
Elemental beings- salamanders
Elemental animals- the coyote, fox, horse, deer, wild cats, praying mantis, scorpion, sharks, hawks, and crickets
Stones- amber, citrine, smoky crystals, bloodstone, carnelian
Metals- gold, brass, iron and steel.

Fire rules spells and rituals dealing with success, sex, illness, protection, legal matters, competitions, strength, and energy.

WATER- A Feminine element
Direction- west
Color-blue
Elemental beings- undines and mermaids
Elemental animals- all sea mammals and birds, fish, night creatures, shell fish, frogs, and the raven.
Stones- river rocks, amethyst, coral, seashells, aquamarine

Metals- silver and copper

Water rules spells and rituals dealing with love, friendship, meditation, healing, dreams, childbirth, clairvoyance and purification.

PLANETARY

Moon- Reveals goddess mysteries, rules spells and rituals dealing with women's health, the home, children, prophetic dreams, reincarnation, sleep, and emotional healing.

Sun- Reveals god mysteries, rules spells and rituals dealing physical health, employment, leadership, prosperity, money, the performing arts and celebrity, self confidence, and new ventures.

Mercury- Rules spells and rituals dealing with the intellect, communications written or spoken, teaching and learning, travel, diplomacy, influencing others.

Venus- Rules spells and rituals dealing with inner and outer beauty, love, romance, family, friendship, gardening, peace, happiness, fertility the creative arts, and sexuality.

Mars- Rules spells and rituals dealing with passion, force, power, lust, courage, will, the military, physical strength, machinery, and competition.

Jupiter- Rules spells and rituals dealing with money, prosperity, success, legal judgments, luck, friendship, financial investments, social gatherings, ambition, and the seeking and granting of favors.

Saturn- Rules spells and rituals dealing with land and real estate, past lives, self defeating behaviors, uncovering lies and losses, and protection from psychic attack.

Uranus- Unexpected changes, higher consciousness, metaphysics, new inventions, regathering scattered energies, clairvoyance, freedom, and independence.

Neptune- Rules spells and rituals dealing with inner vision and perception, intuition, dreams, divination, chaos, confusion and revolution.

Pluto- Rules spells and rituals dealing with death, transformations, astral travel, the otherworld, materializations, transfigurations, and metamorphosis.

DAILY CORRESPONDENCES

Sunday- Ruled by the Sun. Rules spells and rituals dealing with power, prosperity, health, banishing evil and exorcism.

Monday- Ruled by the Moon. Rules spells and rituals dealing with intuition, dreams, psychic ability, female fertility, and the Goddess.

Tuesday- Ruled by Mars. Rules spells and rituals dealing with courage, energy, physical strength, and banishing negativity.

Wednesday- Ruled by Mercury. Rules spells and rituals dealing with divination, communications, knowledge, wisdom, and study.

Thursday- Ruled by Jupiter. Rules spells and rituals dealing with luck, wealth, healing, male fertility, and legal matters.

Friday- Ruled by Venus. Rules spells and rituals dealing with love, sex, marriage, fertility and friendship.

Saturday- Ruled by Saturn. Rules spells and rituals dealing with psychic ability, meditation, and communication with spirits.

MOON PHASE CORRESPONDENCES

● **New Moon-** New Moon magick begins on the day of the new moon to three-and-a-half days after. Use the energy of the new moon for new ventures and new beginnings. Also use the new moon for love spells, job hunting, and healing.

◐ **Waxing Moon-** The waxing moon begins seven to fourteen days after the new moon. Use the waxing moon for constructive magick, such as love spells, magick for wealth and success, courage, friendship, luck or good health.

○ **Full Moon-** A powerful energy for rituals of prophecy, divination and protection. Any spell work that requires extra energy, such as finding a new job or healing serious conditions, is best begun during the full moon. Also for love, gaining sacred knowledge, legal matters, attracting money and prophetic dreams.

◑ **Waning Moon-** Begin waning moon magick three-and-a-half to ten-and-a-half days after the full moon. The waning moon is used for banishing negativity, for curing addictions, and illness.

● **Dark Moon-** The energy of the dark moon is useful for working magick against attackers, and for understanding your own angers and passions. Also for rituals designed to bring justice to bear in very negative situations.

The Moon spends a day or two each month in each of the twelve signs of the zodiac. The sign the moon is transiting through can be used to good advantage during spell work.

Moon in Aries- A good time to perform spells related to jobs and all new projects related to money. Also a good time to perform lust spells, and to develop strength and courage. This is not a good moon for performing divination.

Moon in Taurus- This moon is excellent for spell work related to love, creativity, and inner peace. Spells done at this time take the longest to manifest, but the results will be very long lasting and stable.

Moon in Gemini- The perfect time for spells dealing with communications, healing, and unhexing. Be careful, the moon in Gemini can be unpredictable and unstable.

Moon in Cancer- Excellent for any spell involving the home, fertility, children, or divination.

Moon in Leo- Spells involving leadership, prosperity, fame and career are best done in Leo, but do not perform any spells involving love, or any other emotion, as Leo may actually counteract it.

Moon in Virgo- This moon ensures a spell which involves meticulous detail, especially spells involving education, healing, and stability.

Moon in Libra- Excellent for working a spell with a partner, and for magick involving marriage, couples, partnership, peace, and fairness.

Moon in Scorpio- Use this energy for exploring mysteries, the occult, divination, and sex magick.

Moon in Sagittarius- This is an excellent time to experiment with new techniques, but it is not a good time for psychic work or divination.

Moon in Capricorn- Perfect for spells to manifest life's basic needs, and for stability.

Moon in Aquarius- The best time to work on behalf of others, but consciously stay focused on your heart to maintain a higher consciousness with others, and to avoid selfish motives.

Moon in Pisces- Perfect for divination and psychic work, past life regressions, and communication with spirits.

●☽☽☽◐◐○○○○●◐☾☾●

HERBAL CORRESPONDENCES

Why Are Herbs Used In Magick?

Herbs are used in magick for their 'vibrations' or 'essences'. What does this mean? Herbs, like people, have gender, are ruled by a planet, an element, and are often sacred to a God or Goddess. This is known in Wicca as the herbal correspondence, and it is an important element in Wiccan magick spells. Growing and nurturing herbs in your own magickal garden can give you the advantage of having your own energies already influencing the plant. A plant such as Angelica, ruled by the Sun, will then have all of the influence of the Sun and fire, along with your own personal energies.

Ways to use Herbs

Charms and sachets - Fill a small bag, of the correct color or material, with herbs to make a charm or sachet. You can carry the charm with you, hang it in the house or car, bury or burn it, depending on the purpose of the spell you are performing.

Poppets – You can carve a root into a doll made in the image of the person for which you are working magick, or to represent a person you wish to attract into your life. Poppets may also be carved of wood, wax, or made of cloth, and stuffed with herbs appropriate for the spell.

Incense- Herbs can be burned as ritual incense, such as the sage smudge used to clear negative vibrations from a space.

Bath- Make a sachet, and place it in your ritual or healing bath. Fragrant herbs like lavender make a very relaxing bath, and you can use certain herbs to alleviate skin and other conditions, such as using eucalyptus in a bath when you have a cold or flu.

Oils- Place herbs in an oil, let them steep for a few days, then strain.

You can make anointing oils for you ritual work, beauty oils for your hair, skin and nails (try coconut or jojoba), or flavor oils for cooking and seasoning, such as steeping rosemary or sage in olive oil.

Teas- Use herbs to make teas for healing illness. Some herbs can be used to mildly alter consciousness, such as valerian or kava kava which can facilitate trance like states.

Smoking- You can make herbal smoking mixtures to facilitate altered states of consciousness.

In spell work, herbs can be sprinkled or placed around or within boundaries (such as your home, car, altar, or magick circle) to define a 'territory' for your magick to work. Of course, you can always use flavorful herbs in cooking and seasoning your food. There are many healthful benefits, and they taste great! Always give all plant life respect, where ever you are- remember, the word "weed" is simply a value judgment. Dandelion, for instance, has many, many healing and nutritional qualities which are extremely beneficial not only to the wildlife which feeds on it, but to you, too! Learn to recognize the herbs around you- even in a city, there are many wonderful herbs growing wild, which you can gather and use. Herbs are Nature's gift- use them with wisdom and joy!

LIST OF 117 HERBS

PLEASE NOTE, NONE OF THESE STATEMENTS ARE MEANT TO DIAGNOSE OR CURE ANY ILLNESS, AND ARE FOR INFORMATION ONLY. THE FDA DOES NOT SUPPORT THESE STATEMENTS. Disclaimer made, you can get most of these herbs at Wejee's Metaphysical Superstore at www.wejees.com

ANGELICA ROOT
Sun Fire Masculine
Medicinal Uses: Angelica got it's name during the Great Plagues of Europe- a monk had a dream of an Angel, telling him this herb could

cure the plague. Today, Angelica is valued as a stimulant for the digestive system. It is a good remedy for gas, colic, and acid indigestion. It also is valuable in the treatment of lung diseases, coughs, and colds. It relieves buildup of phlegm due to asthma and bronchitis. Angelica is invigorating to the entire body, and can be used as a tonic for added physical vitality and mental well being. It can also be use to cleanse wounds. **Use with caution Large doses can negatively affect blood pressure, heart, and respiration. If pregnant, can stimulate menstruation, and used to dispel after birth.**

Magickal Uses: Use in protection and exorcism incense, and also carry the root in a blue pouch as a protective talisman. Add to bath to remove hexes. Smoking the leaves causes visions. Angelica protects by both creating a barrier against negative energy, and by filling it's user with positive, radiant energy. Removes curses, hexes, or spells that have been cast against you. Enhances the aura, gives a joyful outlook on life. Burn sun-dried herbs while you announce your desire and retain it in your mind.

ARNICA
Saturn Water Male

Medicinal Uses: It has been used in Europe for hundreds of years to externally reduce bruising and swelling, and to shorten recovery after physical trauma. Use externally in herb baths, and in ointments for chapped lips and irritated nasal passages, for bruises, sprains, dislocations, rheumatism, and skin inflammation. **CAUTION- It should not be taken internally as it is an irritant and can be poisonous.**

Magickal Uses: Use in spells of protection, and invisibility.

ASTRAGALUS ROOT
Mercury Air Male

Medicinal Uses: A very potent herb for strengthening the immune system- it is believed that astragalus works at a very deep level; in the bone marrow, directly enhancing T-cell need. Used function. Astragalus is also very rich in polysaccharides, the basic nutrient that our body's during a serious illness, chemotherapy or during recovery from surgery, it will not only strengthen the body's natural ability to fight off disease and recover, it will also nourish it, and also help to nourish exhausted adrenal glands.. It is a potent adaptogenic herb, also helping to detoxify the liver, help prevent coronary heart disease with it's anti-clotting properties, and increases the flow of bile and digestive fluids.

Magickal Uses: Burn while scrying, especially when the issue has to do with health. Carry as a charm for good health and strength.

BALSAM FIR NEEDLES
Jupiter Water Feminine

Medicinal Uses: Balsam fir is an antiseptic and stimulant, and used for chest infections such as bronchitis, and urinary tract conditions such as cystitis and frequent urination. Externally, balsam fir was rubbed on the chest or applied as a plaster for respiratory infections.

Magickal Uses: Burning fir can aid in divination, prophetics dreams and psychic powers, and it can also be used to attract the aid and power of dragons.

BARBERRY
Mars Earth Feminine

Medicinal Uses: Useful for many liver and gall bladder problems, hepatitis, and cirrhosis. Especially good for jaundice,and to normalize the liver's secretions. It also aids in reducing an inflamed spleen. Barberry also dilates the blood vessels, and can help to reduce blood pressure. It strengthens the body, and is a stimulating herb. Barberry is a very powerful and healing herb for the liver and spleen.

Magickal Uses: Spiritual cleansing, atonement, freedom from the negativity and control of others.

BEARBERRY - UVA URSI

Jupiter Fire Masculine

Medicinal Use: Used for kidney and bladder infections, and kidney stones. It soothes renal and urinary inflammation. It also has an antiseptic effect on the urinary tract. It also helps to balance the Ph of overly acidic urine. It also has a sedative and relaxing effect on the urinary tract, thus reducing frequent urination. It can also help to dissolve kidney stones. Used as a hot bath, it can sooth hemorrhoids. It aids in reducing sugar in the blood, thus is helpful in the control of diabetes. Strengthens the heart muscle, used as a tonic, and helps disorders of the spleen, liver, pancreas, and small intestines. Used as a diuretic. Good for female disorders. Also used in bronchitis, gonorrhea, diarrhea, and to stop bleeding. *It is not necessary to drink the tea for long periods, because acute symptoms generally will disappear within a few days with treatment of bearberry leaf tea.*

Magickal Uses: Native Americans mixed it with tobacco to create the smoking mixture called "Kinnikinnick". Use in spells requiring the element of fire.

BLESSED THISTLE

Mars Fire Masculine

Medicinal Uses: An herb with many uses; Blessed Thistle strengthens the heart and lungs, and it also aids the brain and memory by increasing oxygen in the brain. It also helps to relieve headaches, especially due to menopause, and is a hormone balancer. Also useful for menstrual cramps and hormone related acne. Also a digestive tonic. *Do not take large amounts during pregnancy.*

Magickal Uses: Purification, hex-breaking, protection from evil- removes from the self unwanted influences, particularly of malevolent intent. Brings strength and protection. Strew to cleanse buildings or rooms, beneficial in healing spells.

BUCKEYE
Jupiter Fire Masculine

Magickal Uses: Carried whole, anointed with money oil, or wrap a dollar bill around it, anoint it in money oil, and carry it close to your money for constant increase. Buckeyes are very lucky, and are associated with wealth and divination.

Medicinal Uses: Folklore claims it protects against arthritis when carried in your pocket.

BURDOCK
Venus Water Feminine

Medicinal Uses: Also known as gobo, or "Poor-man's potatoes", it is an important food in Japan, known for it's many healing properties. Traditionally used in Europe, India and China to treat respiratory disorders, abscesses, joint pain, urinary problems and to stimulating cellular regeneration, detoxification and cleansing. Burdock is one of the best herbal blood purifiers for illnesses such as rheumatism and arthritis, chronic infections and skin diseases. It is rich in iron and other minerals.

Magickal Uses: Used in protection incenses and for healing, especially the feet. Carry as a protection sachet or burn for purification of the room, rinse with a root decoction for ridding oneself of a gloomy feeling about yourself or others.

BRAMBLE (BLACKBERRY) LEAF
Venus Water Feminine

Medicinal Use: A mild tea can be used to treat diarreah, especially in children. It is also a highly effective diuretic. It has been chewed in the Middle East since Biblical times to treat bleeding gums.

Magickal Use: Powerful herb of protection and used in invocations to the goddess Brigit, who presides over healing, poetry, sacred wells, and smithcraft. Also used to attract wealth. If twined into a wreath with rowan and ivy, will keep away evil spirits. Plaited around a grave to keep the ghost from rising. Thought to cure various ailments if the sick would walk under an archway of bramble rooted at each end. A bramble patch is a favorite hiding place for faerie folk, use to invoke and attract faerie spirits.

CACAO

Venus Water Feminine

The Aztec's Food of the Gods. An aphrodisiac, a mild euphoric, and helps to heal depression. Also rich in antioxidants. It is extremely effective in love potions and spells. Cacao is a required offering during Day of the Dead, can be used to appease restless spirits, or attract passed loved ones during seance.

CALENDULA

Sun Fire Masculine

Medicinal Uses: Calendula heals wounds as well as internal and external ulcers. It is an antiseptic, and improves blood flow to the affected area. As an antifungal agent, it can be used to treat athlete's foot, ringworm, and candida. The tincture applied neat to cold sores encourages healing . Calendula cream is good for acne and diaper rash. An infusion is good for digestion and relieves colitis and symptoms of menopause.

Magickal Uses: Sprinkle at your door to prevent evil from entering the house, and under your bed to prevent bad dreams or possession. Use to honor and assuage the dead, to attract and honor gods of the Sun, and general good favor, luck and prosperity.

CAMELLIA

Moon Water Feminine

Magickal Uses: Brings riches and luxury, expresses gratitude. Place fresh blossoms in water on altar during ritual to attract money and prosperity. Used in traditional Chinese medicine for treating skin conditions.

CAROB

Mars Fire Masculine

Often used as a chocolate substitute, but though the flavor is similar, the correspondances are opposite. Useful for protection and prosperity (the dried pods were once used as currency). Can be burned as an incense to attract spirit helpers and familiars, or to deter poltergeists.

CATNIP

Water Venus Femininae

Medicinal Uses: Catnip tea will calm the nerves and aid a good night's sleep. Catnip enemas will quickly reduce a fever, and also calm a spastic colon. It also releases gas from the bowels. An old folk remedies is to chew to relieve a toothache.

Magickal Uses: Animal magick and healing pets, increases psychic bond with animals. Use as a tea for happiness and relaxation. Can also be used during meditation, increases psychic abilities. Useful in love magick- try burning dried leaves
for love wishes.

CEDAR TIPS

Sun Fire Masculine

Magickal Uses: Healing, purification, money, protection, love. Cedar smoke is purifying, and can cure nightmares. Keep cedar in your wallet or purse to attract money, or use in money incense. It can also be used in love sachets, or burned to induce psychic powers. Use to draw Earth energy and grounding.

Medicinal Uses: No real healing benefits, but the fragrant tips are popular for adding a smoked flavor to fish and meats when cooked with them. Cedar is also used to make sweet-smelling cabinets, garden and pet bedding, potpourris, and drawer and closet sachets.

CHAMOMILE
Sun Water Masculine

Medicinal and Other Uses: Use as a tea for happiness, relaxation and to cure insomnia. Useful in the treatment of aches and pains in muscles and joints, and it is also useful for indigestion, upset stomach, menstrual cramps, as an anti-inflammatory, and antispasmodic. Rinse light colored hair in chamomile tea to accentuate blonde highlights.

Magickal Uses: Use to attract money, useful as an amulet to attract prosperity. Use in sleep and meditation incense. Prepares the body and mind for magick. Add to a bath or use to wash your face and hair to attract love. Bathe children in chamomile tea to protect from the evil eye, useful in breaking curses cast against you.

CHICKWEED
Moon Water Feminine

Medicinal Uses: For centuries, it was used as a health tonic for domestic birds; try sprinkling it in with their seed. Contains Vitamins A, B, C and fatty acids. Aids in nutrient absorption. A good, all around tonic and nutritious herb, also helps the digestive and respiratory systems, lowers fever. The Chippewa Indians used chickweed as an eye wash and wound poultice.

Magickal Uses: Useful in Moon magick. A good herb for those who work with animal magick, particularly birds.

CINNAMON
Sun Fire Masculine

Medicinal Uses: Anti-bacterial and anti-fungal; was use for centuries as a food preservative, and the Egyptians included it in their embalming mixtures. Works against botulism, E-coli, staph, and candida albicans. Recent studies have discovered that cinnamon has a very positive effect on the blood sugar, an is useful in the control of diabetes.

Magickal Uses: Spirituality, Success, Healing, Power, Psychic Powers, Lust, Protection, Love. Burn cinnamon as an incense or use in sachets and spells for healing, money-drawing, psychic powers, and protection. Mix with frankincense, myrrh and sandalwood for a strong protection incense to be burned every day. A male aphrodisiac.

CLOVES

Jupiter Fire Masculine

Medicinal Uses: Cloves are useful for nausea, flatulence, poor indigestion, infections, dyspepsia, and toothache. Clove oil is also highly antiseptic- the active component of cloves is eugenol, which is known to help kill bacteria and viruses- cloves can help kill several strains of staphylococcus bacteria. Cloves promote sweating with fevers, colds, and flu.

Magickal Uses: Protection, exorcism, love, money, and good luck. Use in incense to attract money, drive away negativity, purify, gain luck or stop gossip. Wear to attract the opposite sex or for protection. Carry it to repel negative energies, also said to protect babies in their cribs if hung over them on a string.

COLTSFOOT

Venus Water Feminine

Medicinal Uses: A soothing expectorant and anti-spasmodic, which can be used to treat bronchitis, whooping cough, asthma, and chronic emphysema. *Caution: Do not use if pregnant or nursing!*

Magickal Uses: Add to love sachets and love spells of all kinds, and use in spells for peace and tranquility. Smoke the leaves to aid in obtaining visions.

COMFREY LEAF

Air Saturn Feminine

Medicinal Uses: Very nutritious, contains almost 35% protein. Excellent for healing sprains, strains, fractures and sores. Also soothes an upset stomach. It is used externally for psoriasis and other skin afflictions. It contains allantoin, which speeds the development of new cell growth. It is excellent for closing and healing wounds, and also for stopping internal bleeding and hemorrhaging.

Magickal Uses: A strong herb for protection against any type of negativity, especially when traveling, and particularly for protection in the astral realms.

DAMIANA

Mars Fire Masculine

Medicinal Use: Damiana was called Mizib-coc by the Maya, and use for asthma, lung problems, dizziness and a general body cleanser. In Mexico, Damiana is mostly used to treat female problems- it helps to balance the hormones, an strengthen the reproductive organs. It is particularly useful during menopause. It is also very useful in male impotency.

Magickal Uses: Sex Magick, Lust, Love, Visions. Use in lust spells. Use in love baths. Burn to enhance visions. Damiana can be prepared in a tea for use in sex magick. It is a mild aphrodisiac and produces a marijuana-like euphoria. It can also be made into a liqueur or be smoked. Damiana is very good for enchanting a male lover. Some say Damiana tea is the best thing for hangovers. Use caution with this herb.

DANDELION LEAF

Jupiter Air Masculine

Medicinal Uses: Potassium rich, and a strong diuretic herb, dandelion will not delete the body's potassium levels like pharmaceutical diuretics. Dandelion is also a strong liver detoxifier. Fresh dandelion is very high in Vitamin A, calcium, and many other nutrients. It is very nutritious, and makes a good addition to salads. Vegetarian pets, such as birds, rodents, rabbits and tortoises also love and benefit greatly from fresh dandelion as a regular part of their diet. Dandelion is also an important component in anti-cancer herbal remedies.

Magickal Uses: Divination, Wishes, Calling Spirits. Use the root in a tea to promote psychic powers. Used in Samhain rituals. Sleep

Protection, Healing. Use in dream pillows and sachets, the leaves and flowers are used in a tea for healing.

DEAD SEA SALT

Saturn Earth Masculine

Medicinal Use: The benefits of bathing in the Dead Sea were well known in ancient times. The famous Greek physician Galen knew that that Dead Sea water was good for the treatment of arthritis, eczema, muscle pain, rheumatism, psoriasis, and, that it also relieved tension, and resulted in soft, silky skin. The Roman historian Flavius wrote "The Dead Sea cannot be praised too highly...travelers take as much of this salt as they are able to home with them, because it heals the human body, and is therefore used in many medicines." Dead Sea salts are rich in just about every mineral, and it is believed that the therapeutic properties of the Dead Sea are largely due to the healthy amounts of magnesium, potassium and bromide.

Magickal Uses: Prosperity, protection, purification, consecration of ritual tools. Sprinkle a few grains around your sacred space to clear it of any unpleasant presences. Some ancient rituals call for pouring dry salt into a receptacle of water to symbolize the dissolving of evil.

DEVIL'S SHOESTRING

Jupiter Fire Masculine

Magickal Uses: Uses include protection, luck, especially good for attracting a raise or new job, and all magick related to jobs and employment.

Medicinal Uses: TOXIC, DO NOT CONSUME.

ECHINACEA

Jupiter Fire Masculine

Medicinal Uses: It is a powerful antiviral- it stimulates the immune system by stimulating the production of white blood cells. Also a very effective anti-inflammatory and natural antibiotic. One of the most potent herbs for speeding recovery from sickness. A potent blood detoxifier and lymphatic cleanser.

Magickal Uses: Can be used with any type of spell-it's power is to add strength to any type of magickal working, but it is especially good in money drawing spells. The dried flowers may be burned as incense. Use as an offering to spirit guides.

ELDERBERRIES

Venus Water Feminine

Medicinal Uses: May be used as a diaphoretic to break fevers, urinary complaints, edema, rheumatic complaints, colds and flu symptoms and muscle pain.

Magickal Uses: Wear an amulet of elder to ward off attackers, and hang in the doorway to ward off evil. Use in protection spells of all kinds. Use elderberries to fulfill your most lighthearted wishes, attracts fairies.

EUCALYPTUS LEAF

Air Moon Feminine

Medicinal Uses: Excellent as a steam for colds and flu-; it kills germs, infections, and eases lung congestion. Can be used as a poultice in decaying, gangrenous or cancerous wounds. Use as a plaster over the lungs or on the back to relieve congestion.

Magickal Uses: Attracts healing vibrations and protection. Use to purify and cleanse any space of unwanted energies. Also useful in dream and sleep pillows.

EUCALYPTUS PODS AND BERRIES

Air Moon Feminine

Exotic and unusual in appearance, Eucalyptus pods and berries are potent in volitile and fragrant oils, and very hard in texture. They make a wonderfully healing and purifying incense, and also are a nice addition to healing potpourri and spell bags.

EYEBRIGHT POWDER

Sun Air Masculine

Medicinal Uses: It has been used since ancient times to make a very soothing eyewash- very good for 'computer eyes'! Also good for blepharitis, cataracts, common cold, conjunctivitis, both as an eye wash and tea. Also good for colds and flu. Beneficial and soothing to the mucous membranes. When sprayed into the nose, it can relieve sneezing fits.

Magickal Uses: A visionary herb and good for clairvoyant works. Magickally, it works to create change internally, shifting attitude from negative to a positive serenity.

FENNEL SEED

Mercury Fire Masculine

Healing, longevity, courage, vitality, virility and strength. Use for protection spells of all kinds. Prevents curses, possession and negativity problems. Use for purification. Gives strength, courage and longevity. Delicious flavor, purifies breath, aids digestion and weight loss.

FEVERFEW

Venus Water Feminine

Medicinal Uses: Excellent daily treatment for migraine headaches- eases inflammation and constriction of the blood vessels in the head, reduces sensitivity to light and nausea. Traditionally used in Europe since the Middle Ages to reduce fever.

Magickal Uses: Include in charms or sachets for love and protection. Also a strong herb for health and spiritual healing. Use as a tea to ward off sickness and bolster the immune system. Protects travelers, keep it in your suitcase or car the next time you travel.

FIG

Jupiter Fire Masculine

Fertility, love spells- excellent ingredient in spell bags. Divination.

Sacred to Dionysus, Juno and many others. Recommended for a Beltane altar. If placed on the doorstep before leaving it will ensure you will arrive home safely.

FLAX SEED

Mercury Fire Masculine

Medicinal Uses: Flax seed is one of nature's richest plant sources of essential fatty acids and is rich in Omega-3. Omega-3 fatty acids help lower cholesterol and blood triglycerides, prevent blood clots which may result in strokes, heart attacks and thromboses. Increased energy, healing, PMS relief.

Magickal Uses: Use to keep the peace at home- place flax seed in a bowl to absorb negative energy. Useful in healing and protection spells. Also, carry flax seeds in your wallet or purse to attract money.

GALANGAL ROOT

Mars Fire Masculine

Medicinal Uses: St. Hildegard of Bingen so highly revered galangal, she called it "The spice of life," and wrote that it had been given by God to protect against illness. It appears in many of Hildegard's formulas. It is primarily used to stimulate digestion and to treat stomach problems, including indigestion, flatulence, upset stomach, gastritis, , nausea, heartburn and diarrhea.

Magickal Uses: Psychic abilities, luck, money. For courage, strength, and for avoiding legal problems. Worn or carried, it protects its bearer and draws good luck. In China, it is worn as a charm to ward off illness. Placed in a sachet of leather with silver, it brings money. Powdered galangal is burned to break spells and curses. It is also carried or sprinkled around the home to promote lust. Worn, galangal aids psychic development and guards the bearer's health. A mild hallucinogen--eat about three inches of the root for this effect. Use caution with this plant.

GINGKO BILOBA

Mercury Air Feminine

Medicinal Uses: Gingko is the oldest variety of tree alive today. It is a very hardy tree- a Gingko was the only tree to survive the nuclear blast in Hiroshima, and that ree is alive today. Gingko is an herb of longevity. Ginkgo is effective in the treatment of innsufficient blood flow, particularly in the legs and brain. Ginkgo has been shown to improve glucose utilization within the brain, and to improve alertness by increasing the brain`s alpha waves, and decreasing theta. It is used to treat conditions such as varicose veins. After 8 weeks to 6 months, male impotence can be relieved by increasing blood flow to the erectile tissue. Gingko also has powerful anti-oxidant properties, and has been shown to inhibit free radicals. One of its main healing properties is its ability to increase tissue oxygenation.

Magickal Uses: Gingko is an aphrodisiac and a fertility herb. It is used in spells of longevity and immortality. Gingko seeds can be substituted for Lotus seeds at weddings and feasts. The wood can be carved into amulets and charms and carried as a healing talisman. Gingko is very useful in ritual healing, and is considered by some to be the sacred Tree of Life. Due to the age of this species, it is considered an elder among trees and having a high spirit energy. The nuts, when dried, may be used to represent male fertility. This plant is useful in all creative work and may be included in a Handfasting.

GINSENG POWDER

Sun Fire Masculine

Medicinal Uses: Ginseng is an adaptogen, having a tonic effect on the pituitary gland, and stimulating the adrenals. It helps the body cope with stress. It can lower blood pressure and cholesterol. Ginseng is particularly beneficial to men, having the effect of increasing testosterone. For this reason, women should not take large amounts of ginseng, or over an extended period of time. While men will benefit from taking it daily, women should only use it occasionally, such as while recovering from physical stress.

Magickal Uses: Rejuvenation, longevity and sexual potency. Use the root in spells to attract love, keep healthy, draw money and ensure sexual potency. Carry to enhance beauty. Burn to break curses or ward off evil spirits. Make into a lust-enhancing tea.

GINGER ROOT
Mars Fire Masculine

Medicinal Uses: Ginger tea is a very effective treatment for nausea, morning and motion sickness. It aids in digestion, relieves gas, and removes excess mucous from the respiratory system. It is warming and stimulating to the body. It may help to prevent strokes and harening of the arteries. For increasing the flow of blood, "chi" energy, and it can increase perspiration. Use ginger tea is used for colds, flu, coughs, and hangovers.

Magickal Uses: Love, money success and power. Eat before magickal workings to increase your power. Useful in love spells. Grow ginger near your home or sprinkle dried ginger in your pocket or wallet to attract money. Ginger root can be a good substitute for mandrake root, and can be used to make poppets.

HAZELNUT
Mercury Air Masculine

Magickal Uses: Spells of healing, protection, luck, clairvoyance, divination, inspiration, wisdom, defense, fertility, wishes. Hazel is an ancient Celtic tree of wisdom, inspiration, and poetry. In Celtic tradition, the Salmon of Knowledge is said to eat the 9 nuts of poetic wisdom dropped into its sacred pool from the hazel tree growing beside it. Ancient Irish tales tell of poets and seers "gaining nuts of Wisdom," a metaphor for heightened states of consciousness; this belief may have root in a potent brew – hazelmead- made from hazelnuts that caused visions. To enlist the aid of plant fairies, string hazelnuts on a cord and hang up in your house or ritual room.

HAZEL WOOD

Mercury Air Masculine

Healing, protection, luck, clairvoyance, divination, inspiration, wisdom, defense, fertility, wishes. In Celtic tradition, the Salmon of Knowledge is said to eat the 9 nuts of poetic wisdom dropped into its sacred pool from the hazel tree growing beside it. The Hazel tree provided shade, protection and baskets. In Europe and North America, hazel is commonly used for 'water-witching' - the art of finding water with a forked stick. Magically, hazel wood is used to gain knowledge, wisdom and poetic inspiration.

HAWTHORN BERRIES

Mars Fire Masculine

Medicinal Uses: Hawthorn is beneficial to the heart due to its ability to increase the ability of the heart to use oxygen. It increases enzyme metabolism in the heart musle, and acts as a mild coronary and vasodialator. Hawthorn is a valubable cardiac tonic beneficial to all heart conditions. Both the flowers and the berries are astringent and a decoction of these will help ease sore throats. It also can decrease restlessness and insomnia.

Magickal Uses: The hawthorn tree is believed to have been the Crown of Thorns placed upon Christ's head, and is sacred in the Christian tradition. It is used to increase fertility and is incorporated into marriage rituals. Use in protection sachets. The leaves can be used to maintain chastity. Used in protection sachets. Hawthorn has been used by witches for centuries, and many rituals can be performed underneath the thorn. Hawthorn is the seat of the old wild magick and was used to decorate may poles. Entering into a relationship with Hawthorn will bring adventure and chaos into your life.

HEAL ALL

Venus Earth Feminine

Medicinal Uses: Heal All (also known as Prunella) is a very old healing herb of European origin, which as spread to many parts of the world. It is an astringent which can be used to stop bleeding, both internal and external. . An infusion is said to be effective with most internal ailments. It is also useful for excessive menstrual flow, hemorrhoids and diarrhea. Heal All is antibiotic and antiseptic. It is used in gargles to relieve sore throat and ulcerations in the mouth, and to stop infections from spreading. I speeds up the healing of wounds, cuts, bruises, burns, ulcers, and sores. It is also believed to reduce scarring. It can reduce lymphatic congestion and has been used to relieve swollen glands. The latest research has shown that Heal All shows promise as an herb to heal herpes and combat HIV.

Magickal Uses: Good luck and money spells. Proclaimed as a Holy herb thought to cure all ailments of man or beast, and to drive away the devil and demons.

HIBISCUS FLOWER

Venus Water Feminine

Medicinal Uses: Soothes nerves, antispasmodic. The tea tart citrusy tea aids digestion, and sweetens the breath. A wash is helpful with itchy skin.

Magickal Uses: Useful as an aphrodisiac and in love spells. Also use to induce dreams, enhance psychic ability and divination.

HIGH JOHN

Mars Fire Masculine

Magickal Uses: Very versatile and powerful herb- increases the strength of any spell. Love prosperity, success, happiness, hex breaking, protection, legal matters. Medicinal Uses: TOXIC, DO NOT CONSUME!

HOLLY LEAF

Mars Fire Masculine

Magickal Uses: Luck, dream magick. An excellent protective herb, keeps away lightning, poison, evil spirits, and other malign forces. The wood is used for all magickal tools as it will enhance any wish you have. A powerful protection.

Medicinal Uses: *Do not consume, toxic. For ritual use only.*

HOPS

Mars Air Masculine

Medicinal Uses: Aids digestion, and is a mild sedative for insomnia. Hops poultice is used for abscesses, boils, tumors, and pain. Honey combined with Hops is good for bronchitis. Hops has antibacterial and antimicrobial effects.

Magickal Uses: Use in healing incenses and spells. Put the flowers inside your pillow to induce sleep, and the tea also helps with sleep. Also drink the tea after magickal practices, to help balance and refocus your energy back to ordinary reality. Use in healing sachets and amulets. Also burned during healing prayers.

HOREHOUND

Mercury Earth Masculine

Medicinal Uses: The leaves and stems are used in candies, cough drops and syrups. Used to treat asthma, coughs, colds, bronchitis, sore throats, and skin irritations. Also used as a diaphoretic, diuretic, expectorant, laxative, stimulant, and stomachic.

Magickal Uses: Use as a tea to increase energy and strength, both physically and mentally- it increases concentration and focus. Carry or burn for protection wishes. Called the "Seed of Horus" by the Ancient Egyptians, it is excellent for blessing one's home. Gather flowering Horehound and tie it with a ribbon, then hang it in your home to keep it free from negative energies.

HYSSOP

Jupiter Fire Masculine

Medicinal Uses: Hyssop is an ancient herb, used sine biblical times as a cathartic. Prepared as a tea, hyssop will soothe colic, improve digestion and eliminate flatulence. It is healing to the digestive membranes. It is an excellent nerve tonic, and also helps one to build up strength after an illness. It is recommended for coughs, colds, flu, and as a gargle for sore throats. Recently, hyssop has been shown to have antiviral properties.

Magickal Uses: An excellent purifying herb. Use in purification baths and spells, and strew about a room or ritual spae to cleanse and purify it. Associated with serpents and dragons, and can be burned as an incense to call on dragon energy. Aids in physical and spiritual protection.

JASMINE FLOWERS
Venus Water Feminine

Magickal Uses: Love spells of all kinds, as well as prosperity, divination, psychic dreams, good for charging quartz crystals.

Medicinal Uses: Considered an aphrodisiac and a sedative.

JUNIPER BERRIES
Sun Fire Masculine

Medicinal Uses: The fragrant scent of Juniper was believed to ward off the plague in ancient Europe. It has a long history of use as a diuretic, and more recently, it has been utilized as a remedy ass to ease arthritis and rheumatism. Aids in kidney function, by isting in the removal of uric acid (but if you have kidney damage, avoid Juniper, as it is too stimulating to the kidneys). An excellent blood cleanser. Applied as a poultice to wounds, it can help prevent infection.

Magickal Uses: Useful for protection magick of all kinds. Makes a good incense for protection. It can be burned or carried to enhance psychic powers. Attracts good, healthy energy, and love.

KAVA KAVA
Saturn Water Feminine

Medicinal Uses: Muscle relaxant, also used to reduce stress and anxiety, insomnia and improve circulation. Produces a relaxed and euphoric mood.

Magickal Uses: Uses include an aphrodisiac, a potent sacramental drink, hypnotic, euphoric visions, aids astral work. it aids access to the subconscious.

KELP

Moon Water Feminine

Medicinal Uses: Kelp is seaweed, and is rich in all the minerals and trace elements of the sea. It is high in iodine, and helps regulate an underactive thyroid. Relieves the pain of rheumtism and rheumatic joints. Mineral-rich Kelp is a popular salt substitute. Because the plant's nutrients come in a natural form, they are easily assimilated by the body. It can be used to enhance the flavor of soups, broths, and chowders. A favorite addition to soothing cosmetic baths, it tones, hydrates and clears the skin. Very rich source of natural vitamins and minerals, including essential trace minerals. A great source of Magnesium, Calcium, Phosphorus, Iron, Potassium, 12 vitamins (including A, B1, B2, C, D and E), 21 amino acids and over 60 minerals and trace elements. It is particularly rich in the trace element

Magickal Uses: Offers protection to those at sea. Summons sea spirits and sea winds. Uses in sachets and spells to increase psychic powers. Scrub floors and doors of business with infusion to attract customers and bring good vibes into store. Use in money spells. Fill small jar with whiskey, add kelp, cap tightly and place in kitchen window. Ensures steady flow of money into the household.

LAVENDER

Mercury Air Masculine

Magickal Uses: Sacred to Hecate, the goddess of witchcraft. Useful in love spells of all kinds. Used during handfastings. Also useful in incenses for healing, sleep, scrying and purification. Perfect for use in dream pillows to promote peaceful sleep and prophetic dreams. Use to manifest money or to attract necessities- use caution- if the spell is for a desire rather than a true need, the spell could backfire. Leave around the house for spiritual and emotional protection. Aids in contacting spiritual beings, and protects against the evil eye.

Medicinal and Other Uses: The fragrance is a useful aromatherapy for insomnia, headaches and many other ailments.

LEMON

Moon Water Feminine

Longevity, purification, love, friendship. Add to purification baths. Use in love sachets and spells. Make good poppets. From "Aradia, Gospel of the Witches"-"THE CONJURATION OF THE LEMON AND PINS- A lemon stuck full of pins of different colours always brings good fortune. If you receive as a gift a lemon full of pins of diverse colours, without any black ones among them, it signifies that your life will be perfectly happy and prosperous and joyful. But if some black pins are among them, you may enjoy good fortune and health, yet mingled with troubles which may be of small account."

LEMON BALM

Feminine Moon Water

Medicinal Uses: Most often used for relieving cold and flu symptoms and reducing fever. Strengthens the immune system, and helps to prevent infection and disease. Relaxes and restores the nervous system. It is great to aid sleep, but it is also beneficial for other nerve disorders including fainting, hysteria and migraine headaches.

Magickal Uses: Love, Success, Healing, Happiness and Fertility. Lemon Balm main is primarily used in healing. Use in healing incense, sachets and spells. Carried, it repels illness. It can also be carried to draw love and ensure success. Drink as an infusion to ease emotional pains after a relationship break-up. It drives away depression and increases fertility.

LEMON VERBENA

Mercury Air Masculine

Medicinal Uses: Lemon Verbena has calming and gentle sedative action, and soothes abdominal discomfort. It has a mildly tonic effect upon the nervous system, helps to lift the spirits and depression. It can help during colds an flus, by helping to clear and dry up mucus.

Magickal Uses: Uses include protection, love spells, excites spiritual love, wear to prevent dreams, adds power to charms, use for purification.

LEMONGRASS

Mercury Air Masculine

Medicinal Uses: Try Lemongrass tea before bed to induce sleep. The infusion is also used to loosen and reduce mucous, to treat fevers, cramps, and stress.

Magickal Uses: Refines psychic abilities and mental clarity, use in love spells to induces lust, purification of ritual space and objects.

LICORICE ROOT

Venus Water Feminine

Medicinal Uses: Licorice root is beneficial during menopause, due to it's phytoestrogens. It also induces the adrenals to produce higher levels of cortisone. This can allow the body to handle stress, and bestows a general feeling of well being. Licorice also possesses anti-arthritic properties. Caution: Avoid during pregnancy and nursing, do not use if you are sensitive to estrogen. Avoid if you have high blood pressure.

Magickal Uses: Love spells, fertility, incites passion and increases the libido- the Kama Sutra recommends mixing the tea with milk as an aphrodisiac. Carry to attract love.

LINDEN FLOWER

Jupiter Water Feminine

Magickal Uses: Excellent for love spells, dream pillows, spells for longevity, and for good luck.

Medicinal Uses: Uses include remedy for colds, coughs, sore throats, flu, mild bladder/kidney problems, and as a mouthwash/gargle. DO

NOT USE FOR PROLONGED PERIODS- can lead to heart damage. For occasional use only!

LOBELIA

Saturn Water Feminine

Medicinal Uses: Counteracts spasms in the lungs, and acts as a bronchial dilator. Excellent in cough preparations. It is also a powerful relaxant and cleansing herb. Drink lots of water with Lobelia, to assist in flushing out toxins. ***Caution- excessive use can be toxic.***

Magickal Uses: Spells dealing with overcoming self defeating behaviors, psychic development, protection from psychic attack, and uncovering past lives.

MANDRAKE ROOT

Mercury Fire Masculine

Magickal Uses: Protection, love, money, fertility, health. Mandrake intensifies the magick of any spell. To charge mandrake root with your personal power, sleep with it for three nights during the full moon. A hallucinogen when used in a tea- it has great power as a visionary herb, empowering your visions, and propelling them into manifestation. A whole mandrake root placed in the home will bring protection and prosperity. Carried, it will attract love and courage.

Medicinal Uses: *Mandrake should only be used medicinally be a qualified herbalist. It is easy to overdose on Mandrake, and it is* **TOXIC.**

MARSHMALLOW ROOT

Moon Water Feminine

Medicinal Uses: The demulcent and emollient properties of Marshmallow make it useful in treating inflammation and irritation of the alimentary canal, and of the urinary and respiratory tract. It also makes an excellent poultice, both soothing and healing wounds. It is calcium and vitamin rich, an can be used to enrich and increase mother's milk.

Magickal Uses: Peace, happiness, femininity and love. Use as a tea to develop an appreciation for the small things and natural beauty of life.

MILK THISTLE SEED
Mars Fire Masculine

Medicinal Uses: Contains the flavonoid sylmarin, which has a direct, beneficial effect on liver cells. Very effective liver cleanser, and also aids in the treatment of hepatitis and cirrhosis. It has a protective, rejuvenating and rebuilding effect not only on the liver, but also the gall bladder, spleen and kidneys. It has powerful antioxidant and free radical scavenger action. It is a known remedy against Amanita mushroom poisoning, and counteracts the toxic effects of dry cleaning fluid. Increases breast milk. It has been used medicinally since ancient times. The ancient Greeks used it as a snake bite remedy, and it was mentioned by herbalist Gerard in 1597.

Magickal Uses: The Anglo-Saxons believed that if milk thistle was hung around a man's neck, all snakes in his presence would begin fighting!

MISTLETOE
Sun Air Masculine

Medicinal Uses: Although Mistletoe leaves are reputed to be a remedy for high blood pressure, the U.S. Food and Drug Administration has labeled this herb "unsafe" and does not approve of its use in treating any illnesses. It was been used in Medieval times for epilepsy, nervous disorders and "St. Vitus dance". It is also a folk remedy for cancer. Use Caution: *The berries are highly toxic, and the leaves can also be toxic.*

Magickal Uses: A fertility herb, an herb of consecration, love, immortality, protection, and an aphrodisiac. great for protection spells.

MORNING GLORY BLOSSOMS
Neptune Water Masculine

Magickal Uses: Happiness, peace, visions. Place under your pillow to stop nightmares and induce beneficial psychic dreams. Sacred to the Aztecs. **Do not consume, toxic.**

MOSS

Jupiter Earth Masculine

Luck, Money. To ensure good luck (especially with money), carry any type of moss removed from a gravestone. A natural wonder, Oak Moss belongs to the element Earth, growing on barks of trees, with a gray suede like appearance. Use this sweet smelling "moss" in Prosperity spells, Gnome magic and spells to Mother Earth. Use in "Witch Bottles" for home & business. Oak Moss attracts Male lust, placing a sachet of Oak Moss in bra When MALE lover is near.

MUGWORT

Venus Earth Feminine

Medicinal Uses: Mugwort is used to slow heavy menstrual bleeding, menstrual cramps, uterine bleeding, and vaginal pain. Crushed fresh leaves can cure warts. It is an antidote for many poisonous mushrooms. Can improve digestion, relieve constipation and liver function. Mugwort place in clothing help protect against moths.

Magickal Uses: Use in dream pillows for prophetic dreams. Burn with sandalwood or wormwood in scrying rituals. Drink as a tea sweetened with honey before divination. The plain tea can also be used to wash crystal balls and magick mirrors. Leaves of mugwort can be placed around these to aid in scrying.

MULLEIN

Saturn Fire Feminine

Medicinal Uses: Useful as an expectorant to clear and heal the lungs, stops diarrhea and soothes hemeroids. During the Civil War, the Confederates used mullein to treat respiratory problems when conventional medicines ran out. It has been used for centuries as a treatment for the symptoms of tuberculosis. It will clear the lungs and relieve spasms, treat lymphatic congestion. Mullein will also strengthen nasal tissue, and allow for freer breathing.

Magickal Uses: Protection and courage. Keeps away demons and nightmares while sleeping, also protects against wild animals. Useful in protection and exorcism spells. Invokes spirits, use on scrying tools to aid divination. This plant is the Original Witch's torch, used to illuminate spells and rites.

MUSTARD SEED

Mars Fire Masculine

Medicinal Uses: Mustard plasters have been used since ancient times to relieve chest congestion. It warms the skin, and breaks up mucous to allow for freer breathing. Mustard plasters can also relieve arthritis and rheumatism when applied to joints. It can also relieve digestive problems.

Magickal Uses: Fertility, protection, mental power. Ancient talisman, symbolizing faith that change can happen. Keeps lovers faithful. Sprinkle mustard seed on your doorstep for protection, and bury it in front of the door to keep supernatural beings and ghosts away from your home.

NETTLES

Mars Fire Masculine

Medicinal Uses: Highly nutritious for anemia, alkalizing the body, treating skin disorders and allergies, and gout. Nettles is a good treatment for dandruff. Dialates the blood vessels, and also cleanses the digestive system.

Magickal Uses: Nettle was cultivated in Scotland beginning in the Bronze Age, for its durable, linen-like fiber. Carry to remove a curse and send it back, or sprinkle around the house to keep out evil. Use in purification baths. One of the nine sacred herbs of the Anglo-Saxons.

NUTMEG

Jupiter Fire Masculine

Magickal Uses: Luck, money and health. Carry for good luck, and to strengthen clairvoyant powers. Use in money and prosperity spells. A hallucinogen when made into a tea. ***TOXIC in large doses! Take no more than a pinch!***

OAT STRAW

Venus Earth Feminine

Medicinal Uses: Very calming to the nerves. Excellent for treating skin conditions such as itching and irritation, or even gout. Supports and soothes the nervous system, helps build healthy bones, skin, hair and nails.

Magickal Uses: Money and prosperity spells, also fertility spells.

OLIVE LEAF

Sun Fire Masculine

Medicinal Uses: Olive leaf is a powerful antibiotic, with both antiviral and antifungal properties. Olive leaf supports the immune system, eliminating harmful bacteria, without harming beneficial bacteria. It can stimulate an immune response in which healthy cells ingest harmful microorganisms. Contains oleuropein and several types of flavonoids, including rutin, apigenin, luteolin.

Magickal Uses: Healing, fertility, potency, protection, and peace. Sacred to many gods and goddesses throughout the ancient Mediterranean world, the Olive branch to this day is a symbol of peace and harmony. Olive leaves can ensure female fertility, and sexual potency in men.

ORANGE PEEL

Sun Fire Masculine

Medicinal Uses: Orange Peel is also a source of pectin, an indigestible carbohydrate that stimulates the growth of probiotic bacteria in the large intestine. These bacteria help prevent food-borne pathogens. Orange Peel has also been shown to aid in the prevention of indigestion, lower cholesterol, and help in the digestion of fatty foods. Orange Peel has been studied as an anti-cancer agent. Supplementing with Orange Peel Powder is a healthy way to increase Vitamin C intake, thus improving overall health in regards to the increased immunity to cold and flu that Vitamin C provides, as well as aiding digestion and preventing food-related illnesses.

Magickal Uses: Love, Divination, Luck, Money. Use the dried peel and seeds in love sachets. Use the flowers in sachets for wedding happiness. Use orange peel in prosperity incenses and spells. Use the peel in Solar incenses.

ORRIS ROOT

Venus Water Feminine

Medicinal Uses: It has been used for respiratory diseases, it also has anti-spasmodic and anti-ulcer properties. Good for headaches, constipation and the thyroid gland. DO NOT USE during pregnancy!

Magickal Uses: Love, protection, divination. Use to find and hold love- a powder made from the root is used as a love drawing powder. Protection from evil spirits. Roots and leaves hung in the house, and added to the bath are good for personal protection.

OSHA ROOT

Mercury Air Masculine

Medicinal Uses: A native of the high of the Rocky Mountains, the root of the osha plant is a traditional Native American treatment for indigestion and upper respiratory infections. Ancient Chinese physicians used plants like osha to "open the interstices" or sweat out a respiratory infection. Like its Chinese cousin ligusticum, Osha will induce sweating, thought to prevent the development of a full-blown cold or flu. Osha is also used to help coughs become productive. Like other bitter herbs, osha stimulates appetite.

Magickal Uses: Purification rites. Spells and rituals involved in developing new ideas, communication and influencing others, and psychic development. Carry an Osha root while taking tests or while public speaking.

PASSION FLOWER

Venus Water Feminine

Medicinal Uses: Calming and soothing, promotes emotional balance, aid in sleep. Use to relieve nerve pain and hysteria. Calms hyperactivity.

Magickal Uses: The Passion Flower gained it's name from 17th Century Jesuit explorers of the New World- to them, the finely cut crown in the center of the flower looked like the Crown of Thorns Jesus wore during the Passion. Magickally, passion flower promotes emotional balance, peace, attracts friendship and prosperity. Heightens libido, use in love spells.

PATCHOULI LEAF

Sun Earth Feminine

Magickal Uses: Uses include reversal spells, clairvoyance, divination, passion, love, sex magick, manifest prosperity, and physical strength.
Medicinal Uses: No known uses.

PAU D`ARCO

Pluto Fire Masculine

Medicinal Uses: The active ingredient is xyloidin, a very potent antibiotic. Also an anti-fungal, antiseptic, anti-swelling agent, anti-inflammatory anti-bacterial, and anti-viral. Used to treat chronic candida. Hospitals in South America have successfully used it to inhibit the growth of ulcers and tumors. Potent tonic, and a powerful blood and cell regenerator, stimulating natural defenses and revitalizing the body. It is also a sedative, an analgesic, and a diuretic.

Magickal Uses: Works best during the energy of the waning Moon- a remedy can best be empowered by drawing down the Moon directly into the herb.

PENNYROYAL

Mars Fire Masculine

Medicinal Uses: The tea is often used as a diaphoretic to inducing sweating to aid in eliminating toxins from the body, and it also as a carminative to relieve gas, stimulate digestion and to relieve nausea. Used in a steamer, it acts as a decongestant and an expectorant, helping to remove excess mucus from the lungs. Used as an insect repellent against fleas, ants, and other pests. *CAUTION: stimulates menustration when consumed or used vaginally, and can induce miscarriage and abortion.*

Magickal Uses: Carry in a green bag to attract money, and to aid in business transactions. Burn for protection during meditation and astral travel. Useful for blocking negative thoughts cast against you-carry when dealing with negative vibrations of all kinds.

PEPPERMINT

Mercury Fire Masculine

Medicinal Uses: Very useful for stomach upset and heartburn, nausea, and to ease congestion during colds and flu.

Magickal Uses: Purification, sleep, love, healing, and psychic powers. Promotes sleep and visionary dreams. Use in healing and purification baths. Burn as a winter incense.

PLANTAIN LEAF

Venus Earth Masculine

Medicinal Uses: An anti-toxic, anti-inflammatory and expectorant. Useful in lung disorders. It is antimicrobial and it is said to stimulate the healing process, and to stop bleeding. Its also used for asthma, bed-wetting, bronchitis, bruise, chronic skin disorders, cough, dermatitis, diarrhea, hemorrhoids, inflammation, insect bites, bee stings, sores, sore throat, and wounds.

Magickal Uses: One of the Nine Sacred Herbs of the Anglo-Saxons. Can be used to increase the strength of any spell, especially those of healing and protection.

POMEGRANATE
Venus Water Feminine

Medicinal Uses: Good source of anti-oxidants when fresh.

Magickal Uses: Given as a gift, may bestow abundance and wishes. May be used to decorate the temple or altar. Brings love, happiness, fertility and prosperity.

RASPBERRY LEAF
Venus Water Feminine

Medicinal Uses: Raspberry leaves have been used to treat diarrhea. In midwifery, raspberry has been connected to female health, including pregnancy. During childbirth, hemorrhaging can be prevented, false labor pains are reduced, and the uterine muscles regulated during delivery. Raspberry leaf tea is rich in

iron, and can enrich the colostrum found in mother's milk. It is also a remedy for excessive menstrual flow.

Magickal Uses: Protection, healing, and love. Calming, it promotes sleep and visions.

RED CLOVER
Mercury Air Masculine

Medicinal Uses: A nutritious herb, blood building and purifying. Contains many trace minerals, vitamins and nutrients. Used in many anti-cancer formulas and teas. A very versatile and beneficial herb.

Magickal Uses: Protection, Money, Love, Fidelity, Exorcism, Success, Clairvoyance, Beauty. Brings good luck. Induces clairvoyant powers. Use for rituals to enhance beauty and youth.

RED CEDAR
Sun Fire Masculine

Magickal Uses: Healing, purification, money, protection, love. Cedar smoke is purifying and can cure nightmares. Keep cedar in your wallet or purse to attract money, and use in money incense. It can also be used in love sachets or burned to induce psychic powers. Use to draw Earth energy and grounding.

Medicinal and other uses: The fragrant tips are popular for adding a smoked flavor to fish and meats when cooked with them. Cedar is also used to make sweet-smelling cabinets, garden and pet bedding, potpourris, and drawer and closet sachets.

ROSE PETALS

Venus Water Feminine

Medicinal Uses: Helps clear away headaches, dizziness, mouth sores and menstrual cramps. Heart and nerve tonic. The earliest known gardening was the planting of roses along the most traveled paths of Neolithic nomads.

Magickal Uses: Love, psychic powers, healing, luck, protection. Use in love spells of all kinds. Drink rose tea before bedtime for prophetic dreams. Domestic peace and happiness, promotes joy of giving.

ROSE HIPS

Venus Water Feminine

Medicinal Uses: Rose hips are very high in Vitamin C. Rose hips also contain A, B, E, and K, organic acids and pectin, and has high concentrations of iron.

Magickal Uses: The hips are strung like beads and worn to attract love. A woman should eat rose hips (dried or fresh) during their menstrual period. A woman's lover should gather roses for this purpose. The earliest known gardening was the planting of roses along the most traveled routes of early nomadic humans.

ROSEMARY

Sun Fire Masculine

Medicinal Uses: During WWII in French hospitals, rosemary and juniper berries were burned to help kill germs. Rosemary tea sharpens the senses, alleviates headaches, nervous systems and to improve memory. Circulatory, digestive and nerve stimulant. Treats stomach aches and halitosis. Use as a hair rinse to enhance dark shades of hair.

Magickal Uses: To the ancient Greeks, rosemary was believed to strengthen the memory, and students wore rosemary in their hair while they studied. Protection, love, lust, mental powers, exorcism, purification, healing, sleep, youth. Burn to purify and cleanse. Use in love and lust incenses and potions.

SAGE

Jupiter Air Masculine

Medicinal Uses: Heals wounds, aids weak digestion, eases muscle and joint pain, colds and fever. Can slow persperation, and relieve the "night sweats" of menopause. Also a natural deodorant. Dries up breast milk. Calms the nerves, and is a powerful anti-oxidant.

Magickal Uses: In antiquity, sage was thought to be the herbal Saviour of Mankind- it's latin name, "salvia" means saviour. Spells involving immortality, longevity, wisdom, protection, and prosperity. Use in healing and money spells. Use as incense during sacred rituals-walk the smoke to the four corners of the room to repel and rid negative energies and influences. This is especially good when moving into a new home to dispel and purify any "bad vibes" left behind by the previous occupants.

SANDALWOOD CHIPS

Moon Water Feminine

Magickal Uses: An herb of consecration, immortality, and a visionary herb. Often used as an as an aphrodisiac. Used to assist with meditation, trance work, and all forms of divination. It calms the mind and helps one become spiritually focused. Used to increase opportunities and success. Burn as a purifying incense.

Medicinal and other uses: The essential oil has aromatherapy benefits.

SKULLCAP

Saturn Water Feminine

Medicinal Uses: A tranquilizer and a nervine. Scullcap influences the central and sympathetic nervous systems. It will bring about a very relaxed sleep. Most herbalists recommend using Scullcap regularly for best effect. Can help with drug and alcohol detox. Antispasmodic.

Magickal Uses: Use in spells for love, fidelity, relaxation and peace. Calms and centers the mind for magick.

SHAVEGRASS

Saturn Earth Feminine

Medicinal Uses: Also known as Horsetail. Nutritious, helps the body absorb calcium, may help to strengthen bones, hair and nails. Control excess oil on the skin. Diuretic, helps to relieve urinary disorders. Said to help the blood to clot, reduce fevers, reduce nervous tension, and temper an overactive liver.

Magickal Uses: Fertility spells. Also can be used in snake charming!

SCOTCH BROOM LEAF

Mars Air Masculine

A Druid sacred tree. Use in purification and protection spells and scatter to exorcise evil spirits. Burn to calm the wind. The branches are used to make traditional besoms. It is said the tea can induce psychic powers, and it's smoke is a sedative. *Toxic, for Ritual use only!*

SEAWEED

Moon Water Feminine

Medicinal Uses: Kelp is seaweed, and is rich in all the minerals and trace elements of the sea. It is high in iodine, and helps regulate an underactive thyroid. Relieves the pain of rheumtism and rheumatic joints. Mineral-rich Kelp is a popular salt substitute. Because the plant`s nutrients come in a natural form, they are easily assimilated by the body. It can be used to enhance the flavor of soups, broths, and chowders. A favorite addition to soothing cosmetic baths, it tones, hydrates and clears the skin. Very rich source of natural vitamins and minerals, including essential trace minerals. A great source of Magnesium, Calcium, Phosphorus, Iron, Potassium, 12 vitamins (including A, B1, B2, C, D and E), 21 amino acids and over 60 minerals and trace elements.

Magickal Uses: Offers protection to those at sea. Summons sea spirits and sea winds. Uses in sachets and spells to increase psychic powers. Scrub floors and doors of business with infusion to attract customers and bring good vibes into store. Use in money spells. Fill small jar with whiskey, add kelp, cap tightly and place in kitchen window. Ensures steady flow of money into the household.

SLIPPERY ELM

Saturn Earth Feminine

Medicinal Uses: Can be used as a tea for inflammatory bowel or for bronchitis. It is healing and soothing to mucous membranes. Slippery elm's calcium content makes it a good calmative for emotional or nervous problems. As a tonic it is known for its ability to soothe and strengthen the organs, tissues and mucous membranes, especially the lungs and stomach. Antibiotic and anti-microbial effect. It is alleged to revitalize the entire body.

Magickal Uses: Burn to attract propriety, fetility and growth. Use in spells to stop gossip.

SOLOMON'S SEAL

Saturn Water Masculine

Medicinal Uses: Astringent, demulcent, and tonic. A laxative and restorative, and is good in inflammations of the stomach, indigestion, profuse menstruation, lung ailments, general debility, fades bruises, also apply to cuts and sores.

Magickal Uses: An aphrodisiac, an herb of consecration, and an herb of protection. Excellent herb to use when consecrating a ritual room or space for the first time. Use to make and keep oaths.

SPANISH MOSS

Jupiter Earth Masculine

Luck, money, banish poltergeists- To ensure good luck, especially with gambling, carry Spanish moss. Use in "Witch Bottles" for home & business. Place around home, or burn to banish poltergeists.

SPEARMINT

Air Mercury Masculine

Medicinal Uses: Spearmint is used as a flavoring in many dishes, candies, and drinks, and as an ingredient in cosmetics. Medicinally, Spearmint Leaf is similar to Peppermint, though it is considered to be milder. For this reason, Spearmint Leaf has traditionally been used in treating stomachaches in children. Spearmint Leaf is primarily used in digestive problems, including indigestion, flatulence, vomiting, and colic. It has also been used as a mild diuretic, anti-inflammatory, and as a fever reducer.

Magickal Uses: Purification, sleep, love, healing, psychic powers. Promotes sleep and visionary dreams. Use in healing and purification baths. Burn as a winter incense.

SPIRULINA

Moon Water Feminine

Medicinal Uses: Spirulina is a blue-green algae containing complete, balanced protein and a wide range of valuable nutrients. It is considered a "Super Food". Spirulina is a wonderful way to consume high quality, vegetarian protein that is easy on the body- ounce for ounce, it has almost 4 times the protein of beef. It is 70% protein, compared to beef's 18%. In addition to being one of the most nutrient-rich foods on earth, Spirulina is low in fat, calories and carbohydrates. Spirulina is an RNA/DNA balancer, it removes toxins from the body, and it boosts the immune system, and is one of the most complete foods known.

Magickal Uses: Use to summon and connect with the Source of All, with Primal Substance, primeval gods and goddesses.

ST. JOHN'S WORT

Sun Fire Masculine

Medicinal Uses: St. Johns Wort has been used for over 2,000 years as an antiseptic and a calming herb. Used as an herbal remedy for mild to moderate depression, anxiety, and sleep disorders. St. Johns Wort helps support levels of seratonin. Its also used as a digestive aid, pain killer, and to reduce chronic tension headaches.

Magickal Uses: Health, protection, strength, love divination, happiness, and exorcism. A Druid sacred herb. Use in protection and exorcism spells and incenses of all kinds. Use as a tea to treat depression. Use the leaves in a necklace to ward off sickness and tension. Carry to strengthen your courage and conviction. Burn to banish negative thoughts and energies.

STAR ANISE

Jupiter Air Masculine

Medicinal Uses: A stimulant and diuretic. Promotes digestion and to relieves flatulence. Delicious flavor!

Magickal Uses: Protection, purification, youth, psychic powers, luck. Use for protection, meditation and psychic power incenses. Can be used in purification baths. Wards off evil and averts evil eye. A pillow stuffed with anise seeds will keep away nightmares. The tree is planted by the Japanese around temples and on graves as an herb of consecration and protection. The seeds are burned as incense to increase psychic powers, and are also worn as beads for the same purpose. Sometimes star anise is placed on the altar to give it power; one is placed to each of the four directions. It is also carried as a general luck-bringer, and the seeds make excellent pendulums. The tree is often grown near Buddist temples where it is revered.

THISTLE FLOWER

Mars Fire Masculine

Represents courageous defense and deep rooted ideals. Protection spells, also is used to bring spiritual and financial blessings. Carried in an amulet for joy, energy, vitality, and protection. Can be burned as an incense for protection and also to counteract hexing.

THYME

Venus Water Feminine

Medicinal Uses: Thymol, its active ingredient, is a powerful germacide. (Thymol is one of the active, germ killing ingredients in Listerine) Thyme helps to loosen phlegm, combats bronchial spasms, and discourages growth of bacteria. It is a general antispasmodic, helpful in calming coughs. Also useful in uterine and intestine spasms.

Magickal Uses: The name Thyme is derived from the Greek word thymos, which meant strength. For an ancient greek to say someone smelled like thyme was a great compliment! Burn for good health and use in healing spells. Burn as purification incense. Wear to increase psychic powers. Aphrodisiac.

TOBACCO LEAF

Mars Fire Masculine

Sacred to the Native American Tradition. Tobacco ties- wrap tobacco leaves in pieces of white, red, yellow and black cloth, and hang them around the ceremonial space at the 4 cardinal directions. Smoke to allow communication with spirits. Burn as an incense to purify a space. Spirits appreciate offerings of tobacco.

TONKA BEANS

Venus Water Feminine

Magickal Uses: These beans are used for all forms of good luck, be it in finances, love, health or anything else. They can also help keep your spirits up during difficult times. Sometimes the oil from the tonka plant is used, but it`s most commonly the beans. Tonka beans are a common item in Voodoo magick.

Medicinal and other uses: Often used as a vanilla like fragrance in cosmetics, perfumes and tobbacco.

UVA URSI - BEARBERRY

Jupiter Fire Masculine

Medicinal Uses: Used for kidney and bladder infections, and kidney stones. It soothes renal and urinary inflammation. It also has an antiseptic effect on the urinary tract. It also helps to balance the Ph of overly acidic urine. It also has a sedative and relaxing effect on the urinary tract, thus reducing frequent urination. It can also help to dissolve kidney stones. Used as a hot bath, it can sooth hemorrhoids. It aids in reucing sugar in the blood, thus is helpful in the control of diabetes. Strengthens the heart muscle, used as a tonic, and helps disorders of the spleen, liver, pancreas, and small intestines. Used as a diuretic. Good for female disorders. Also used in bronchitis, gonorrhea, diarrhea, and to stop bleeding. *It is not necessary to drink the tea for long periods, because acute symptoms generally will disappear within a few days with treatment of bearberry leaf tea.*

Magickal Uses: Native Americans mixed it with tobacco to create the smoking mixture called "Kinnikinnick". Use in spells requiring the element of fire.

VALERIAN ROOT

Venus Water Feminine

Medicinal Uses: Valerian has been in use since pre-Christian times as a sedative and sleep aid. A muscle relaxant and a potent tranquilizer, useful in treating anxiety, nervous disorders and insomnia. A common misbelief is that Valium s derived from Valerian; this is not true, but Valerian has found use in easing withdrawl symptoms for those with Valium addictions. It works by effecting the central nervous and cerebrospinal systems.

Magickal Uses: Use for dream magick and sleep protection baths. Keep in the home or grow in the garden to aid a harmonious atmosphere. May be used to purify a ritual space. Useful in consecrating incense burners. Drink tea daily, in moderate doses, during times of purification.

VERVAIN
Moon Water Feminine

Medicinal Uses: In medicinal use since Roman times, Vervain does a little good for a lot of things; colds, nerves, gout, skin conditions, painful or irregular periods, expels worms and more. Today, it is mostly used to decongest and cleanse the liver.

Magickal Uses: The Romans used Vervain to purify their homes and temples. The Catholics believe that Vervain staunched Christ's bleeding at the crucifixion, and was given the name, "Herb of the Cross". Protection amulets and spells, purification, aids divination, consecration, love potions and spells, creativity.

WHEATGRASS POWDER
Venus Earth Feminine

Medicinal Uses: Exceptionally rich in vitamins, minerals and all good things! Increases hemoglobin production and rebuilds the blood. Neutralizes toxins, carcinogens, and helps to purify the liver. Improves blood sugar disorders, keeps hair from graying. Improves digestion, removes heavy metals from the body, reduces high blood pressure, and aids in the prevention and curing of cancer. Wheatgrass powder and juice is gluten free!

Magickal Uses: Use for fertility spells, to honor the Goddesses of the Earth, prosperity and health spells.

WHITE SAGE
Jupiter Air Masculine

Medicinal Uses: Heals wounds, aids weak digestion, eases muscle and joint pain, colds and fever. Can slow persperation, and relieve the "night sweats" of menopause. Also a natural deodorant. Dries up breast milk. Calms the nerves, and is a powerful anti-oxidant.

Magickal Uses: In antiquity, sage was thought to be the herbal Saviour of Mankind- it's latin name, "salvia" means saviour. Spells involving immortality, longevity, wisdom, protection, and prosperity. Use in healing and money spells. Use as incense during sacred rituals-walk the smoke to the four corners of the room to repel and rid negative energies and influences. This is especially good when moving into a new home to dispel and purify any "bad vibes" left behind by the previous occupants.

WHITE WILLOW BARK

Moon Water Feminine

Medicinal Uses: White Willow's active ingredient is glucoside salicin, an effective pain reliever similar to aspirin. But while natural White Willow has the same benefits as asprin, it will not have the same harsh side effects. It reduces inflammation and eases muscle and joint pain.

Magickal Uses: Love, divination, protection, and healing. Carry and use in spells to attract love. Use the leaves, bark and wood in healing spells. Burn with sandalwood to conjure spirits. Brings the blessings of the moon into one's life.

WILD CHERRY

Venus Water Feminine

Medicinal Uses: Due to its powerful sedative action, it is used primarily in the treatment of irritating and persistent coughs when increasing expectoration is inappropriate, and thus has a role in the treatment of bronchitis and whooping cough and in the racking cough of debility or convalescence. It can be combined with other herbs to control asthma. Both the cyanogenic glycosides and volatile oil help to improve the digestion, and may be used as a bitter where digestion is sluggish. The cold infusion of the bark may be used as a wash in eye inflammation and as an astringent in diarrhoea.

Magickal Uses: Love spells and divination.

WORMWOOD

Mars Fire Masculine

Medicinal Uses: Useful with stomach disorders, liver and cardiac stimulant, and a classic herb for expelling intestinal worms. It is also helpful in stopping internal bleeding and can counteract some poisonous mushrooms. It is useful for constipation. It promotes mestruation and reduces cramps. CAUTION: Do not give to children!

Magickal Uses: Psychic powers, protection, and summoning spirits. Burn with sandalwood to increase psychic powers or to conjure spirits. Use in divinatory and clairvoyant incenses. Carry for protection. banishes anger and negativity, exorcism.

YARROW FLOWER

Venus Water Feminine

Medicinal Uses: Yarrow's latin name, "Achillea" comes from ancient Greek legend, that says the hero Achilles used Yarrow to bind the wounds of his soldiers during the conquest of Troy. Another version of the story says that it was used to bind Achille's wounded heel. Yarrow does have the ability to stop bleeding and assist with the healing process. Yarrow is a good remedy for colds, it opens the pores, increases warmth and purifies the blood. It aids the liver. It removes uric acid from the blood, thus relieving gout. The Navajo call Yarrow "Life Medicine" and used it chewed to stop tooth aches, and made a tea of the flwoers, which was poured into the ears for ear aches.

Magickal Uses: Use to dispel melancholy, negative energy, lingering sorrow, or depression. Carried as a sachet or amulet, it repels and rids negative influences. Aids in divination. Builds courage to overcome adversity.

Many of the herbs on this list are available at Wejee's Metaphysical SuperStore at www.wejees.com We have both 1-2 oz sizes, and big one pound bags. Wejee's Metaphysical SuperStore also carries a complete selection of books on herbal magick and healing.

ESSENTIAL OILS AND INCENSE

What magick does fragrance possess? It can move our souls, bring back memories, calm our minds, and set the stage for romance. Perhaps the secret lies deep in the most ancient core of our brain- the limbic system. It processes our sense of smell, and also controls our "autonomic" nervous system- our breath, our heartbeat. Scent can affect the autonomic nervous system, causing the breath to deepen and slow, which in turn, calms the heart.

Many illnesses begin in the mind, and the benefit of aromatherapy is that it helps ease the unconscious causes of distress. Aromatherapy utilizes essential oils to stimulate both psychological and physical benefits. Essential oils are not perfume or fragrance oils- they are literally the pure 'essence' of a plant, and are unadulterated by any artificial or chemical ingredients. Not all ready made aromatherapy products labeled with the word "aromatherapy" are pure and natural. Avoid products which use "fragrances" or chemical ingredients. True aromatherapy products will contain only essential oils, and other all natural ingredients.

Essential oils have a rich, natural aroma, which can offer either relaxing or stimulating psychological benefits by triggering the brain (perhaps in the same way pheromones do, by stimulating the release of subtle hormones.) The components of the oils also enter the lungs, and oils applied to the skin absorb into the bloodstream, providing actual physical benefits. But essential oils must be used with care- they are very concentrated, and in pure form, can irritate the skin. They are commonly diluted with 'carrier' oils such as sweet almond, apricot kernel, grapeseed, or jojoba, and stored in brown or blue glass bottles to protect potency.

Essential oils are often blended together to form 'synergies'. Properly blended in the right proportions, synergies can be of greater benefit than the individual oils used separately. That is the art of an aromatherapist, and their special blends are often closely guarded professional secrets.

Experimenting with aromatherapy can be a fun way to add a rich, calming sense of beauty to your life!

LIST OF 35 ESSENTIAL OILS

ANGELICA

Sun Fire Masculine

Alleviates irritated and congested skin, psoriasis. Eases fatigue and stress, aids insight, mediation and contact with Angels.

ANISE

Jupiter Fire Masculine

Aids digestion, antiseptic, eases headaches and respiratory problems, muscle relaxant. Stimulating and uplifting, it balances and clears the mind, aiding clairvoyance and divination.

BERGAMOT

Sun Fire Feminine

Clears oily skin and acne, dermatitis, soothes cold sores, antiseptic, immune system booster. An uplifting and cheerful

fragrance, it works as an anti-depressant. Use for protection and also in drawing prosperity.

CARROT SEED

Jupiter Water Feminine

Excellent for wrinkle smoothing, revitalizing mature skin, and healing eczema and psoriasis. Contains Vitamins A, C, B1, B2. the fragrance is a mood stabilizer, it is vitalizing and uplifting.

CEDARWOOD

Sun Fire Masculine

Balances combination and oily skin, heals acne, rashes, excellent hair and scalp tonic. Eases coughs and bronchitis. Good for grounding, relaxing, and balancing the energies. Attracts prosperity and wealth.

CHAMOMILE

Sun Water Masculine

Soothes acne, sensitive and delicate skin, eczema, heals wounds and burns, eases muscle pain, and an anti-inflammatory. The fragrance is calming and sleep inducing.

CINNAMON

Sun Fire Masculine

Strong antiseptic. Mix with a carrier oil and use topically to aid poor circulation, ease sore muscles, rub on the chest to ease congestion due to colds and flu. A male aphrodisiac, use in love attraction and lust spells. Stimulating and warming, it aids psychic powers and protection.

CLOVE

Jupiter Fire Masculine

Antiseptic, treats colds, flus and nausea. Use to relieve tooth and gum pain. Useful on acne and bruises. Wear to attract the opposite sex, or to repel negativity.

CORIANDER

Mars Fire Masculine

Beneficial for acne, psoriasis, and dermatitis, digestion and circulation. A calming, soothing, and warm fragrance, use to anoint candles during love spells.

CYPRESS

Saturn Earth Feminine

Astringent and antiseptic for oily skin. Helps break up cellulite, and aids circulation. Excellent for relaxation, tension and anger reduction, assists during life transitions- use during times of mourning. An oil of blessing, consecration and protection.

EUCALYPTUS

Moon Air Feminine

Treats fungal infections, cleans wounds, antiseptic, anti-viral, bactericidal, colds, flu, fever. Useful in vaporizers and healing baths. Strengthening, invigorating and uplifting scent.

FENNEL

Mercury Fire Masculine

Treats bruises, cellulite, cellulitis, and asthma. Detoxifying and antiseptic. Encourages courage, strength, and energy, the scent is uplifting and cheerful.

FRANKINCENSE

Sun Fire Masculine

Heals dry and mature skin, heals scars, antiseptic, very rejuvenating. Meditative, calming, and sedative, the rich scent aids in inner guidance. Traditionally used in temple, altar and church incense.

GRAPEFRUIT

Jupiter Water Feminine

Tissue toning, treats congested skin, cellulitis, diuretic, antiseptic. Relieves nervous exhaustion and stress, joyful and energizing fragrance.

HYSSOP

Jupiter Fire Masculine

Very emollient, softens scars. The scent stimulates lymphatic system, and helps relieve emotional grief; add to a bath to create a purified atmosphere. An excellent oil to wear during all types of magical rituals, especially for properity.

JASMINE

Venus Water Feminine

Antiseptic, very hydrating to dry and sensitive skin, softens scars. Aphrodisiac, emotionally warming and

balancing, sweet scent, use to attract love. Also for relaxation, sleep, and meditation.

JUNIPER

Sun Fire Masculine

Skin toning, antispetic, clears oily complexion. Detoxifying, diuretic, eases arthritis, strengthens the immune system. Relieves nervous tension, the fragrance is strengthening and expansive.

LAVENDER

Mercury Air Masculine

Antiseptic, antibacterial, heals burns, scars and wounds, cold sores. Analgesic, antibiotic, eases headaches, decongestant, relieves PMS. Balancing, purifying, uplifting, clean fragrance, aids intuition. Also attracts the opposite sex.

LEMON

Moon Water Feminine

Blood purifier, antiseptic, immune system stimulant. Attracts solar vitality and energy, the fragrance is purifying and brings mental clarity. Attracts spirit guides.

LIME

Sun Water Masculine

Astringent, tonic, restorative, emollient, anti-viral, detoxifying, eases rheumatism. Stimulating, cheerful anti-depressant fragrance.

LINDEN BLOSSOM

Jupiter Water Feminine

Mild astringent, emollient, tonic, antispasmodic, and diuretic. Sweetly sedative and calming, it acts as a nerve regulator.

MYRRH

Moon Water Feminine

Antiseptic, astringent, disinfectant, and revitalizing to the skin. Eases bronchitis, wounds, and flatulence. Energizes the crown chakra, facilitating a connection to the Divine. For purification, protection and hex-breaking.

NEROLI

Jupiter Water Feminine

Revitalizes and rejuvenates mature skin. Antispasmodic and antiseptic. The scent is a sedative, an anti-depressant, and encourages creativity and love.

ORANGE

Jupiter Water Feminine

Heals stretch marks, gentle tonic, detoxifying to stomach and liver. Hypnotic, the scent connects to the inner child, lightening the heart and mind to new possibilities.

PATCHOULI

Sun Earth Masculine

Relieves chapped skin, wrinkles, oily hair and skin. Eases diarrhea, vomiting, stomach pain, headaches and the flu. Frees the spirit, gives peace of mind, and fosters creativity. A grounding scent, and an aphrodisiac- used by men to attract women. It also wards off negativity and evil.

PINE

Sun Air Masculine

Stimulating and refreshing, muscle relaxant, antiseptic, aids circulation, eases aches. Sedative, comforting and calming fragrance.

PEPPERMINT

Mercury Fire Masculine

Treats indigestion and nausea, colds and sore throat, tooth aches, colic and mental fatigue. The invigorating smell promotes visionary dreams, and facilitates change.

ROSE

Venus Water Feminine

Antiseptic, tonic, excellent for wrinkles and dry skin, cell regenerator. The lovely, romantic fragrance is an aphrodisiac- it connects the soul to the heart chakra. Use for love spells of all kinds. Also insures domestic peace.

ROSEMARY

Sun Fire Masculine

Treats acne, oily skin, thinning hair, wounds, antiseptic, rheumatism, sore muscles, bronchitis, colds and headache. The scent is stimulating for both the body and mind, it strengthens mental clarity and awareness during rituals.

ROSEWOOD

Sun Earth Feminine

Tissue regenerator, sensitive skin, tonic, antiseptic, analgesic, calming. The fragrance is emotionally balancing and an anti-depressant.

SANDALWOOD

Moon Water Feminine

Astringent, treats dry skin, eczema, and irritation. Antispasmodic, antiseptic, diuretic. The deep, sweet and woody scent is a sedative, elevating and spiritual, it aids in meditation. Aids in seeing past incarnations.

TEA TREE

Mercury Air Masculine

Effective treatment for acne, cold sores, and insect bites. It has strong antibiotic, antiviral, antifungal, anti-

inflammatory, and antibacterial qualities. The fresh scent revitalizes the mind, especially after shock.

TUBEROSE

Venus Water Feminine

Promotes sensuality, relaxation and euphoria, the sweet smell centers the emotions. Aids divination and love spells.

VERBENA

Venus Earth Feminine

Antiseptic and emollient, it reduces skin swelling, acts as an antispasmodic. The scent is sedating and spiritually uplifting.

YLANG YLANG

Venus water Feminine

Sedative, reduces stress, relieves PMS, acts as an aphrodisiac. The fragrance is exotic and sensual, positively mood altering. Makes its wearer irresistible to the opposite sex.

USES OF COMMON INCENSE

Cedar- Purification and protection, spiritual growth and prosperity, money spells.
Cinnamon- Love, sex magick, psychic ability, and protection.
Copal- Purification and cleansing of ritual space and stones.
Dragon's Blood- Lust, courage, and sexuality.
Frankincense- Protection, spirituality, and consecration of your ritual tools and space.
Jasmine- Love, peace, and prophetic dreams.
Juniper- Exorcism, healing and love magick.
Lavender- Balancing, uplifting, aids intuition.
Myrrh- Healing, protection, consecration of ritual tools and space, meditation.
Nag Champa- Meditation and the creation of sacred space, cleansing the home of negativity. Calming, encourages peace.
Patchouli- Frees the spirit, and fosters creativity. Grounding, and an aphrodisiac.
Pine- Money, purification, and exorcism.
Rose- Love, psychic powers, healing, luck, protection, domestic peace and happiness.
Rosewood- Emotionally balancing and uplifting.
Sage- Spiritual growth, healing, and purification of the home and ritual space.
Sandalwood- Protection, healing, love and spiritual growth.
Vanilla- Love, seduction, mental powers, aphrodisiac.
Ylang Ylang- Love, sensuality, sleep and dreams.

CRYSTALS AND STONES

Crystals carry energy vibrations, and can subtly help to bring the energy vibrations within your body and aura into a healthy and vibrant balance. Quartz, in particular, is uniquely potent and useful- have you ever wondered why quartz crystals wind up in everything from inexpensive wristwatches, to the most advanced technology? The electronics industry is based on the properties of silicon and quartz crystals; these amazing natural minerals organize and regulate electrical energy. Metaphysically, the quartz crystal can be 'programmed' to help clear away negative energy from the aura and re-align the chakra energy centers of the body. Magickally, crystals can be programmed to hold the energy of your desire, and they can charge your spell work and magickal charms with the energy necessary to manifest into physical reality!

Clearing and Programming Crystals

Crystals are a tool, and can act as a storage battery for positive energy. Crystals can be 'programmed' with our thought energy, and act on our subtle energy fields. They also to help to create situations in our lives that will lead us in directions that allow for positive growth and healing.

Clearing a crystal or gem stone is a simple task, and it is a way to insure that there are no left over negative energies from the person who owned it before you. It is a way to personalize your crystal, and create a new energy bond between you and your new gem stone partner. There are many ways to do this, but this is a simple and effective way - make sure you will not be disturbed. Hold your new crystal under running water, and as the water pours over it, close your eyes and imagine all the negative energies are washed away down the drain and out to the vast ocean to be purified by the cycle of life. You can also leave them in the warm Sun, and allow the power of its light purify to the crystal with fire.

To program your new crystal, simply hold it in your hand, close your eyes, then in your imagination, create an image of what you want your crystal or gem stone to help you create. Keep your crystal close to your skin, and when you can not wear it, store it in a special box or bag, which has also been purified and blessed. Fill your crystal companions with love, and you will
receive it back threefold!

Crystals and the Zodiac

Aquarius- hematite, amethyst, amber

Pisces- amethyst, opal, bloodstone, coral, aquamarine, fire opal

Aries- fire agate, aquamarine, bloodstone, citrine, diamond, emerald, jade.

Taurus- carnelian, diamond, blue tourmaline, chrysocolla, rose quartz

Gemini- rutilated quartz, aquamarine, blue sapphire, emerald, jade, pearl

Cancer- moonstone, ruby, carnelian, opal, fire opal

Leo- citrine, amber, garnet, jasper, carnelian, diamond

Virgo- smoky quartz, watermelon tourmaline, amethyst, moss agate, geodes

Libra- rose quartz, tourmaline, bloodstone, citrine, jade, moonstone, opal

Scorpio- turquoise, moldavite, malachite, moonstone, opal, peridot, ruby

Sagitarius- lapis, obsidian, topaz, azurite, chalcedony, smoky quartz, turquoise

Capricorn- tigereye, jade, black tourmaline, green tourmaline, garnet, smoky quartz

Metaphysical Properties of 50 Crystals

Agate- Balances yin/yang energy, and stabilizes the aura. Imparts strength and courage. Opens you to your own innate creative talents.

Amber- Purifies body, mind, and spirit. Balances the electromagnetic flow of the body, and allows for an even
flow of energy. Provides a positive, soothing energy, and spiritualizes the intellect.

Amethyst- A stone of stability, strength, and peace; a very calming energy. Encourages spirituality and contentment, an excellent companion for meditation. Enhances psychic ability.

Amazonite- Fosters Universal love and harmony, by balancing your personal energy with that of the cosmos.

Aventurine- Fosters independence, leadership, and creativity. Balances male and female energies. Aligns the intellectual, physical, emotional, and etheric bodies.

Aquamarine- Assists in spiritual awareness and actualization. Brings courage, stimulates the intellect, and provides protection.

Azurite- Awakens psychic ability, insight, and intuition, by opening the third eye. An excellent companion for clearing the mind during meditation.

Beryl- Provides energy for psychic healing and awareness, plus psychic and physical protection.

Bloodstone- Imparts strength, courage, and the self confidence needed to succeed in business and legal affairs. Attracts wealth, sexual potency, insures victory.

Calcite- This stone is an energy amplifier, excellent for clearing and cleansing the aura. A very calming and centering, peaceful stone.

Carnelian- A healing stone that counteracts feelings of apathy, fear and rage. Fosters peace within and without, imparts self confidence, and inspired verbal and written communication.

Celestite- An excellent companion stone for dream recall and astral travel, helps to develop verbal skills and personal growth.

Chrysocolla- Provides strength and balance. Promotes harmony and attunement with the Earth, purifies the environment.

Citrine- Dissipates negative energy, encouraging warmth, joy, and optimism. Helps to develop psychic powers.

Diamond- Represents purity, perfection, abundance, and inspiration. Imparts courage, strength, sexual prowess, mental and psychic development.

Emerald- Fosters loyalty, emotional sensitivity, harmony, and tranquility. Assists in memory retention and mental clarity. Attracts balance, abundance and prosperity.

Fluorite- Aids stability, order, discernment, and concentration. Aids in the understanding and maintaining of ideals.

Garnet- Fosters commitment, compassion, devotion, love, stability and order. Promotes an even flow of energy.

Geodes- Represents fertility and childbirth, the Earth and the Mother Goddess. Excellent aid to meditation, fosters freedom of the mind and spirit.

Hematite- Excellent for the mind, and for spiritual grounding. A calming and healing stone, aids sleep, meditation and psychic divination.

Jade- Fosters harmony, peace, fidelity, and confidence. Also attracts prosperity and longevity.

Jasper- Provides protection, mental awareness, insight, and spiritual grounding. Encourages physical health and beauty.

Kunzite- Promotes constructive communication, love and peace. Protects and dissolves negativity. Excellent companion stone for meditation.

Kyanite- This amazing stone never needs cleaning or clearing. It has the power to align all chakras. Promotes tranquility, communication, and psychic awareness. Excellent
for meditation and dream recall.

Labradorite- Represents the light of the Universe, and cosmic energy. Fosters intuition and illumination.

Lapis Lazuli- Fosters knowledge, wisdom, and spiritual perfection. Provides protection, and fosters creativity. Brings joy, prosperity and beauty.

Lepidolite- Promotes honesty, stability, hope, and acceptance. Assists during change and transition. Facilitates travel in the astral realms.

Malachite- Facilitates transformation and spiritual development. Clears the way to attaining goals. Excellent companion stone on vision quests.

Moldavite- Provides spiritual clarity, and access to interdimensional realms. Develops psychic abilities, plus mental and emotional balance.

Moonstone- Represents the emotional and intuitive Lunar female energy. Smoothes out rhythms, cycles, and clears a way for destiny to be fulfilled. Attracts love, harmony and light.

Obsidian- Dispels negativity. A grounding, healing, and protective stone. Aids personal insight, and facilitates self growth and change.
Onyx- Very centering, facilitates self-control and intuitive guidance. Assists during the grieving process.

Opal- Facilitates creativity, inspiration, and imagination. Fosters beauty, love, and emotional balance. Brings good luck and prosperity.

Peridot- A healing and protective stone. Allows insight into life changes, and regulates the life cycles.

Petrified Wood- Grounding, provides strength. A stone of transformation.

Pyrite- A symbol of the sun, this stone shields against negative energy, and is a good stone for psychic protection. Enhances the intellect and memory.

Rhodochrosite- Brings peace, calm and emotional balance to mental activity.

Rose Quartz- Empowers and attracts the energies of love, happiness and peace. Encourages healing on all levels.

Ruby- Fosters love, nurturing, spirituality, wealth, and protection. Helps to prevent nightmares.

Rutilated Quartz- Intensifies energy, and stimulates the brain. A stone of inspiration and clairvoyance.

Sapphire- Fosters beauty, and brings love, meditation and peace. Brings prosperity and provides protection. Develops psychic ability and inspiration.

Shiva Lingam Stone- Lingams are only found at the Narmada River high in the mountains of Mandhata, one of the seven sacred holy places of pilgrimage in India. The stones are "Crypto Crystalline Quartz", said to contain the loftiest vibration of all stones on Earth. They emanate a vibration that will purify your altar or home. The stone represents both the male energy of knowledge and the female energy of wisdom.

Smoky Quartz- This stone works to dissolve negativity. It is very grounding and balancing. Excellent companion stone for meditation.

Sodalite- Encourages logic, efficiency, and truthfulness. Reduces stress, and enhances group communication.

Sugilite- Represents and encourages spiritual love, inspiration, and self confidence. Alleviates negative and destructive emotions.

Sunstone- Imbues the aura with energy, health, passion and sexual potency.

Tigereye- An earthy and grounding stone, representing both the sun and the earth. Promotes optimism, insight, common sense and personal power. Attracts good luck, prosperity, and protection.

Topaz- Fosters success, individuality, creativity, and joy. A good companion stone for dieters, it encourages emotional balance and tranquility.

Tourmaline- Inspires understanding, self-confidence, and emotional balance. Fosters friendship, peace, love and prosperity.

Tourmalinated Quartz- A stone of strength and balance. Combines the attributes of tourmaline and quartz.

Turquoise- Creates spiritual attunement, strength, and grounding, an excellent stone for astral travel. Encourages good communication, friendship, and healing.

COLORS

Colors, bright or dark, deep or light, regardless of whether it's a royal blue or a brilliant yellow, color affects us. It's a proven fact that colors have an affect on our intellect, and they invoke different emotional responses. Colors used in magick are similar in that they evoke a response, but keep in mind, response to color is an individual matter, so go with your instincts. The colors must have meaning to you. The magick of colors can be used in many different ways, and the use of colors in magick is only limited to what you want to use the color for.

White- Always burn at least one white candle to symbolize and reinforce contact with pure spirit. White connects to elemental spirits, angels, Gods of Wisdom, divination and prophecy. Purifying and cleansing on all levels, white maintains contact with the higher self and spiritual helpers, aids in aura-healing, truth seeking, consecration, and spiritual enlightenment. Protects against negativity and breaks curses. Useful during exorcism, meditation, and divination. Inspirational and clairvoyant. White can be used as a replacement for any other color.

Yellow- Elemental air. Calls in deities beneficial for trade, travel, knowledge and magick. Aids vitality, change, progress, contacts, communication, and trade. Strengthens confidence, joy, cheerfulness, aids learning, knowledge, mental clarity, concentration, speaking, writing and visualization.

Gold- Spells and rituals dedicated to Sun-deities, solar powers, and masculine energy. Bolsters self confidence and creativity, brings financial success, luxury, and power. Aids in conquering bad habits and addictions.

Orange- Sacred to deities of good luck and good fortune. Encourages personal charm, optimism, success, abundance, and prosperity. A color of feasting and celebration. Aids in achieving business goals and success in legal matters.

Copper or Bronze- Used to call upon Love Goddesses, fosters love and passion, encourages positive relationships in love, friendship or business. Use in spells to achieve career promotions and successful negotiations.

Red- Color of elemental fire, sacred to deities of love, passion, sexuality and war. Bolsters courage, determination and assertiveness. The color of aggression and masculinity. Represents independence, physical strength, competition and conflict. Beneficial for stimulating good health, sexual attraction, potency, passion and fertility.

Magenta- Aids in personal magnetism, and the ability to attract or speed up results in magick. Represents your life purpose.

Pink- Attracts Love Goddesses, encourages softness, tenderness, romance, nurturing, and youth. A color of peace, friendship, femininity, emotional love, and emotional healing.

Green- The color of elemental earth and elemental water. Attracts nature and fertility deities, and Mother goddesses. Use in spells and rituals dedicated to nature, fertility, rejuvenation, recovery, healing, harvest and abundance. Promotes prosperity, harmony and balance in the home. Use for healing rituals involving plants and animals.

Turquoise- Promotes positive changes, intellectual and intuitive insights, inspires inventiveness and originality. The color of renewal, brotherhood, and humanity.

Blue- The color of elemental water and elemental air. Attracts deities of the sea and sky. Promotes peace and tranquility. Inspires truth, wisdom, and justice, promotes understanding and patience, loyalty and honor, sincerity and devotion. Wear as a protection during sleep, especially during astral projection.

Violet- Attracts elemental spirits, angels, and Gods of divination and prophecy. Promotes psychic abilities, counteracts negativity and black magick, useful in hex reversal and divination. Encourages psychic healing, meditation, spirituality and astral projection.

Brown- The color of elemental Earth, represents stability, grounding, protection of the household, family and pets. Promotes healing in animals, finding lost objects, and material wealth. Helps to increase decisiveness and concentration.

Gray- Neutralizes negative energies, putting a stop to destructive and negative action. Hex and curse reversal.

Silver- Sacred to Moon goddesses, represents feminine energy, cycles, rebirth, reincarnation, healing, and emotional stability. Removes or neutralizes negative energy. Aids intuition, dreams, psychic abilities and psychic workings.

Black- The color of elemental earth, sacred to deities of the Underworld. Repels and banishes evil and negativity, use for protection. Facilitates deep meditation.

TREES

Trees were sacred beings to the ancient Celtic peoples of Europe, and many other primal peoples of the Earth. Rooted in the Earth, and reaching upwards towards Heaven, trees are symbolic of the human striving for spiritual perfection, and can serve as role models and spiritual guides. Make friends with the trees around you- they can be great magickal allies, helping to ground and transmit your desires and goals from the Earthly realm out into the Cosmic Consciousness, where your dreams will find their manifestation.

Here is a list of twenty-two familiar trees, along with their magickal correspondences. Their leaves, bark and fruits are valuable herbal ingredients for your spells, their wood is essential for making wands, and as magickal 'familiars' and allies, they are the Kings and Queens of the Earthly forest!

Alder

Saturn Earth Feminine

Represents resurrection and new life, and makes a valuable ally when making a new beginning yourself. The time to honor this tree is in the Spring. A relationship with this tree will foster inner strength, confidence, and self awareness.

Apple

Venus Water Feminine

This tree is the symbol of beauty, innocence and youth. It is the tree of regeneration and eternal life. The apple's most common use is in love spells. The blossoms can be used in sachets, potions, incenses and candles. The apple is one of the foods of the dead, and might be offered to the dead on Samhain. Magick wands that have strong connections with the emotions and love can be made from apple wood.

Ash

Sun Fire Masculine

Represents the Ygdrasill, the Norse Tree of Life and the Universe. The ash represents the union of inner and outer worlds- as the roots grow up from the Earth, and the branches reach towards the Heavens, they manifest together in our world, as the trunk. It is a tree ally that can be used for prophesy and visions. Ash sometimes represents the power which resides in water, and it was believed that a piece of ash carved into a solar cross would protect seafarers. To ward off evil, hang a staff carved of ash over your doorpost. The leaves can be scattered to protect an area, and can be used in protective sachets and spells. Healing wands and brooms can be made from the wood, and poppets can be carved from the roots. Place ash leaves beneath your pillow to induce psychic dreams. Ash leaves can also be carried for general good fortune.

Aspen

Mercury Air Masculine

This tree is ruled by Mercury, and aids in mental awareness and communication. Plant this alert tree of communication and awareness on your land to protect from thieves. An aspen leaf placed under the tongue can make you an eloquent speaker during those frightful times when you must get up and speak in front of a group.

Birch

Venus Water Feminine

The lovely, Celtic Lady of the Woods. The Birch represents rebirth, purification, and is sacred to the Goddess. Its hardiness represents the daily work we all must perform to maintain our daily bread. A friendship with this forest mother will bring joy and inspiration to all our daily, little chores, and is a great spiritual ally for young mothers.

Cedar

Sun Fire masculine

The ancient and venerable Cedar has a long history of participation in sacred ritual, both in the Old World, and New. Burn cedar as a smudge during sacred rituals- walk the smoke around the circle to repel and rid the sacred space of negative energies and influences. Also use cedar as a fuel wood in sacred fires. Cedar smoke is purifying, and can cure nightmares. Keep cedar in your wallet or purse to attract money, and use in money incense. It can also be used in love sachets or burned to induce psychic powers. Use to draw Earth energy and grounding.

Cypress

Saturn Earth Feminine

The Guardian and guide of the Underworld. Cypress is sacred to the gods of Mysteries, and of sorrow. Wear or carry cypress to funerals, for peace of mind during a time of grief. Boughs of cypress can be used for protection in thehome. Carry an amulet carved of the wood to lengthen your life. A healing wand can be made from cypress wood. The root, cones, and leaves are all healing, and the leaves can be burned as an incense. This incense can be used to consecrate ritual objects.

Elder

Venus Water Feminine

The fairy tree- stand or sleep under an elder at Midsummer's Eve to see faeries, elves and gnomes. Wear an amulet of elder to ward off attackers, and hang in the doorway to ward off evil. Use in protection spells of all kinds. Flutes and wands made from elder wood can be used to call forest and other nature spirits. Use elder to fulfill your most lighthearted wishes.

Elm

Saturn Water Feminine

This forest mother is associated with Embla, the first woman in Norse mythology, and the elm is an ally during childbirth. Carry an amulet of elm to attract love, and wands made of elm aid in the healing of feminine health issues.

Eucalyptus

Moon Air Feminine

This graceful mother of the Australian wilderness has great healing properties of all kinds, both physical and spiritual. The leaves kill germs, infections, and ease lung congestion. Wands made of eucalyptus attract healing vibrations and protection. Scatter or burn the leaves to purify and cleanse any space of unwanted energies. Also useful in dream and sleep pillows. Eucalyptus pods and berries are potent in volatile and fragrant oils- they make a wonderfully healing and purifying incense, and also are a nice addition to healing potpourri and spell bags.

Hawthorn

Mars Fire Masculine

A powerful ancient Celtic tree, planted to protect Holy Ground, and also planted at crossroads. Plant hawthorn on your property to protect your home from poltergeists, and other mischievous or malevolent spirits. The wood can be used to make wands and amulets to attract love and fertility.

Hazel

Sun Air Masculine

Hazel is the ancient Celtic tree of wisdom, inspiration, and poetry. In Celtic tradition, the Salmon of Knowledge is said to eat the nine nuts of poetic wisdom dropped into its sacred pool from the hazel tree growing beside it. Irish tales tell of poets and seers "gaining nuts of Wisdom," a metaphor for heightened states of consciousness; this may have root in the potent brew, "hazelmead", made from hazelnuts, and purported to cause visions. To enlist the aid of plant fairies, string hazelnuts on a cord and hang in your house or ritual room. Commonly used for 'water-witching' - the art of finding water with a forked stick. Magically, hazel wood is used to gain knowledge, wisdom and poetic inspiration.

Holly

Mars Fire Masculine

An excellent protective wood, keeps away lightning, poison, evil spirits, and other malignant forces. The wood can be used to make all magickal tools, as its power will enhance any magickal working. A powerful protection from evil and bad luck, holly provides protection during the "dark season" of Winter, thus the tradition of making wreaths of holly during the Yuletide.

Juniper

Sun Fire Masculine

The venerable juniper is a useful ally for protection magick of all kinds, it is an excellent protector when burned as an incense or smudge. It can also be burned or carried to enhance psychic powers. Juniper attracts good, healthy loving energy tthose who befriend it. The berries aid digestion, intestinal cramps, act as a diuretic, eases the pain of arthritis. Planting a juniper provides protection from theft, attract love, good health, and psychic powers.

Linden

Jupiter Water Feminine

Plant a linden to provide protection and foster good luck. Use linden flowers in spells for love. Burn linden wood to protect from ill luck and negative forces.

Magnolia

Venus Earth Feminine

The magnificent beauty of magnolia blossoms are valuable in love spells, particularly those for fidelity. Use a magnolia wand for love, marriage and fertility spells.

Maple

Jupiter Air Male

The maple is native to both Europe and America, but it was never tapped for sugar in Europe. Maple trees attract both money and love; maple syrup can be used in spells and potions, as well as wands made of maple.

Mesquite
Moon Water Feminine

This western tree of the high desert is a survivor; mesquite makes an excellent ally for those in recovery of all kinds. It aids in spiritual awakening, and in the ability to find what one needs to survive, even in the harshest of landscapes. It can awaken your vision to the smallest pleasures and blessings in life. Use mesquite in healing incenses, and use as fuel wood for magickal and visionary fires.

Mimosa
Saturn Water Feminine

This lovely, exotic tree is useful for spells of love, protection, dreams and purification. Try using the fragrant flowers in a dream pillow, or love spell. Use the seeds in a protection charm, and burn the seeds, pods and flowers for purification.

Mulberry
Mercury Air Masculine

Symbolic of a gentle protection and strength; it is the sole home and food to silk worms, who use its essence to weave their incredibly delicate, yet strong, cocoons. Seek out mulberry as an ally during times of withdrawl from worldly demands, and as an ally when making your re-entry. Wands and amulets for attracting wisdom, beauty and lightness can be made of Mulberry.

Myrtle

Venus Water Feminine

The myrtle is a very feminine tree, useful in love spells. Make a charm of myrtle to increase fertility, and to preserve youth and beauty. Keep a branch of Myrtle in your home to maintain peace.

Oak

Sun Fire Male

The King of the Forest. Druids and others worshiped and taught the Mysteries under the oaks- the oak assists in rites of magickal protection, power collection, power focusing, and spells of stability. An oak tree is an excellent ally in learning magick- if you can, study the craft while sitting with your oak allies. Burn oak leaves for purification. Carry acorns for immortality and longevity, for fertility, and for protection against illness. Carry an amulet made of the wood for protection and good luck, and powerful wands of protection are made of Oak.

Olive

Sun Fire Masculine

Sacred to many gods and goddesses throughout the ancient world, the olive branch is still a symbol of peace, harmony and abundance. Olive leaves can ensure female fertility, and sexual potency in men. It is a powerful antibiotic, with both antiviral and antifungal properties. Olive leaf supports the immune system, eliminating harmful bacteria, without effecting beneficial bacteria. Wands and amulets of healing, peace, and fertility can be carved from olive wood,
and boughs of olive hung over doorways provide protection and peace to the home.

Pine

Sun Air Masculine

Known in ancient times as "the sweetest of woods". Its needles are a valuable source of vitamin C and can loosen a tight chest. The scent of

Pine is useful in the alleviation of guilt. Burn pine for strength, and to reverse negative energies. The cones are a powerful protection amulet against evil. Useful in making wands and amulets for sacred wisdom, prosperity, fertility, and healing.

Rowan

Sun Fire Male

A rowan walking stick protects the traveler, insuring a safe trip home. Carry to increase psychic powers. In divination, it is used to ground the senses. Use to make wands and dowsing rods. Use the leaves and berries in divination and psychic power incenses. Use in healing sachets and spells. A cross of rowan twigs is carried for protection.

Willow

Moon Water Feminine

Sitting peacefully in a grove of graceful, feminine willows will provide artistic inspiration, prophesy, and eloquence. Sacred to Goddesses of the Moon, a willow is an invaluable ally to creative artists of all kinds. The willow symbolizes flexibility and growth. Carry a charm made of willow to attract love, use to make wands of artistic inspiration. Use the leaves, bark and wood in healing and love spells.

Yew

Mars Fire Masculine

An important tree during the Winter Solstice and sacred to deities of death and rebirth. Boughs of yew were laid upon graves, as a reminder that death was only a pause before rebirth. The yew is a tree of longevity- extremely ancient yews can be found in churchyards all over the British Isles. Meditating under a yew may be used to enhance magical and psychic abilities, and to induce visions. All parts of the tree are poisonous- do not consume.

SPELLS

A Sampling of Simple Spells
for Love, Money and Protection

When working spells, always consider the ethical implications- "... and harm ye none" is the basic tenet of the Wiccan Rede, and that means no curses, hexes or revenge! Remember, the best revenge is a life well spent, so instead of working against others, simply work to gain the best life possible for yourself, separate from any difficult situations or people you are currently experiencing. This is especially true if you cast a love spell at a specific person, and it is simply not meant to be. The spell may work for a while, but it will eventually backfire. We all have our own free will, so do not try to hold onto people or situations that are really not right for you. You really can't change others, you can only work to change yourself! Remember the Wiccan rule of three- whatever you do, will come back to you, amplified three times. Working as a good witch is just good sense!

> **"Mind the Threefold Law you should,**
>
> **three times bad and three times good.**

> **Eight words the Wiccan Rede fulfill:**
>
> **An ye harm none, do what ye will."**

You can get everything you need to do these spells at Wejee's Metaphysical Superstore at www.wejees.com We also have ready to go spell kits with everything you will need to get started with Wiccan Magick!

Prophetic Dream Pillow

This spell will create a magickally charged pillow stuffed with dream inducing herbs. Here's a clever suggestion- sew a pocket into your dream pillow to keep you dream journal and pen!

By the light of a Full Moon, anoint a white candle with jasmine oil. Light it, and solely by the light of this candle, sew a small pillow by hand, while repeating silently:

by the light of the Moon
I dream
by the light of my soul
I see
with understanding and light
I dream through the night

Stuff the finished pillow with the herbs hibiscus, jasmine flower, and dandelion leaf, and pillow stuffing (preferably natural and organic cotton or wool). Sprinkle it with jasmine oil, and let the candle burn all the way down. Sweet dreams!

Before we get to the love Spells, a few words on the subject of 'Soul Mates' So what is a soul mate? First and foremost, it should be a person with good personal boundaries, and it will be a person who's energy compliments, not conflicts, with your own. But 'compliment' does not mean 'merge'. Please consider this - you probably won't be able to recognize what compliments rather than conflicts with your own energy until you learn to recognize your own spiritual boundaries, have released your emotional and mental addictions and obsessions, and are able to rest comfortably in your own 'psychic skin', or aura.

Although the feeling of instant psychic recognition and magickal attraction feels like 'soul mate', it's often not. It could be Karmic. This person could be here to literally test the boundaries of your spiritual development, to challenge you to know who *you* are, and to be true to *yourself*. This may be beneficial for a time, but these relationships must be released if you are to advance along the path, and have a possibility of finding a truly comfortable Soul Mate in the here and now!

Love Attraction Spell

You will need:
A pink candle
Rose oil
Dried jasmine flowers
Dried rose petals
Dried hibiscus flower
Rose quartz crystal
Wood box

The day before the New Moon, place the dried flowers in the wood box. After cleansing it, bury the crystal in the dried herbs, and hide it in a safe place. This will begin the process of charging the crystal.

On the evening of the New Moon, anoint the candle with rose oil. Light it. Now, anoint the crystal with rose oil, and begin massaging yourself with it, starting at your feet. While doing this, repeat this incantation:

I am infused with the light of love
I radiate love from my center
magnetized with positive energy
like attracts like
my lover is drawn to me
like magick!

When you are thoroughly massaged, your aura will be positively charged and cleansed. Now, take the rose quartz in your hands, and repeat:

*This gem is infused with light
it radiates light from it's center
magnetized with positive energy
like attracts like
my crystal attracts love like magick!*

When thoroughly charged, replace the crystal in the box, and place it under your bed. Let the candle burn all the way down.

Use the rose oil and incantation regularly, and massage yourself with the crystal, to keep yourself positively charged. You can also carry it as a charm.

Flower Power Love Spell
You will need:
Red votive candle
A passion flower, hibiscus or rose bush
Spring water
House plant food
Ylang ylang or rose oil
Rose or ylang ylang incense
A large, pretty flower plant
A permanent marker pen
A journal

On the evening of the Full Moon, set up an area where you can leave the ceremonial items undisturbed, overnight. Place your plant in the center. Contemplate this plant, admire it, and with love repeat this Earth prayer:

I am grounded and rooted firmly in the earth, like this plant. I draw nourishing energy from the Earth, the Sun, the Air, and Water, like this plant. The elements of life sustain me.

Add the recommended amount of plant food to the spring water, and say this Water prayer:

Cool water, symbol of emotion, sometimes still, sometimes turbulent, but always moving. Like a great river, the deep ocean, the gentle stream, I will not grow stagnant, and I ask the powers that protect and guide me to bless and purify this offering.

Place this water to the left of your plant. Inside the pot, with a permanent marker, write your name. Then write this incantation:

I am a living, growing being, just like this plant, always changing, always growing, reaching for my own fertile, emotional maturity. Reaching Heavenwards, I nourish and nurture this beautiful plant, the symbol of the love I have to give, and the love I deserve to receive. Everyday the love in my life grows a little bigger, a little greener, more lush, and soon it will blossom and bear fruit. I am grateful to God and the Universe for the love I receive from this plant I care for, from the people in my life, both familiar and new, from animals and nature, and most importantly from myself.

Make sure you get a pot big enough to write all this!
Now, take the red votive candle, and anoint it with the oil. Dab some of the oil on the incense, and on yourself, too. Place the candle on a small saucer or candle holder, and then put it inside the pot, and set it to the right of the plant. As you light the candle, say the Fire prayer:

Candle flame, element of fire, burn away the aloneness I no longer need.

Allow yourself to relax, and clear your mind. (I suggest you use the meditation techniques on this website.) Imagine yourself to be like the candle- feel the line of energy running up through your center, like a wick, and feel the aura about your head like a flame. Then repeat the incantation you wrote in the pot. This is your personal incantation. Say it over until you feel satisfied, then light the incense with the candle. Say this Air prayer with a sense of joy:

My prayers, my hopes, my dreams are carried like smoke on the wind, to Heaven. The element of Air is everywhere, yet unseen, and like the Goddess, it sustains, and connects, all life. My breath is my connection to all life and the Goddess, and I remember to breathe life in deeply, as my constant, sustaining prayer.

Spend the rest of your evening quietly, play gentle music, relax, and contemplate the meaning of the words you have said for the spell. Let the candle burn down all the way. PLEASE, make sure it is in a place where nothing can catch on fire!

In the morning, after you've had breakfast and feel awake, remove the candle from the pot, and plant your plant. As you are working, admire the beauty of the plant, smell its fragrance, feel and smell the soil, and say the Earth prayer. Say your incantation as you work. Say the Water prayer as you water the plant with the spring water. Find a nice, sunny place for your plant, and say the Air prayer. Then light some more incense, say the Fire prayer, and be done with the ritual. It is very important that you feel finished!

As you sustain and grow your plant, so you will sustain and grow the spell. But it is VERY IMPORTANT that you do not obsess on it! Just know that it is happening, and allow yourself to relax.

Make a habit of wearing a little of the rose or ylang ylang oil as a perfume, and when you really need to relax, drink a cup of herb tea, and contemplate the prayers. Don't think about the prayers, or obsessively repeat them in your head, but contemplate, which means to meditate on the meaning behind the words. Use the prayers as positive affirmations.

When your plant is mature enough, you can harvest a few flowers to make tea. If your plant dies, don't worry, or take it as a bad omen! It could be the plant has absorbed and removed a lot of negativity. Just repeat the ritual.

Know that you and your life will now begin to change, perhaps quickly, maybe slowly, but change it will! Be patient, the amount of emotional healing you require will determine how quickly the spell will work. Spells don't work overnight- it might be a week, a month, maybe even a year before you really notice a difference, so be patient with yourself. Use the journal to vent your feelings, good and bad, and use it to define the qualities of the person you hope to meet.

Soul Mate Attraction Spell
You will need:
Dried rose buds
Dried hibiscus flowers
Dried lavender flowers
Dried rosemary
Rose oil
Lavender oil
A shiva lingam stone
(if unavailable, use a rose quartz or amethyst egg)
a pair of white taper candles
A red charm bag

On the evening of the Full Moon, anoint one candle with rose oil, to represent the feminine and one with lavender, to represent the masculine. Surround the female candle with rose and hibiscus, the male with rosemary and lavender; join the two circles in a figure eight, and place the stone in the middle.

Calm yourself, breathe deeply, and call into the candles the spirit of the Great God and Goddess, petitioning the Divine Couple to infuse flower and stone with radiant energy and warmth. Pray deeply for them to bless the spell, and to grace you with the love you deserve. Light the candles, releasing the blessing of the God and Goddess, while you repeat this incantation:

I shine
like a beacon
a light in the darkness
my love will find me!

Now anoint your left side with rose oil, your right with lavender, joining at your third eye, while repeating:

in inner unity
I am radiant
glowing bright
my twin flame
reflects my light, shining bright

Sweep the herbs and the lingam into the charm bag. It is now charged to attract your soul mate! Keep it with you, or in your bedroom. Know that your work is over, and feel free to be yourself!

To Heal the Hurt of Lost Love
You will need:
A yin/yang shaped candle
A blue votive candle
Pen and paper
Jasmine flowers
Hibiscus flowers
Rose buds
Yarrow
Lavender
Chamomile
Valerian root

144

An amethyst pyramid
Jasper worry stone
A red charm bag
A picture of your lover
Lavender oil
Ylang Ylang oil
A charcoal burner
Frankincense resin
A wooden box

First, make a tea with 1/2 teaspoon each of the chamomile and valerian, to help clear your mind of negative thoughts. The first step is to cleanse the negative charge of abandonment from your aura. Anoint the blue votive with lavender oil, and light it. Next, run a hot bath using the lavender, and while bathing, repeat this incantation:

I wash my spirit clean today
I cleanse myself of pain
my heart is freed from yesterday
I wash it down the drain

Get out, dry off, and rub some lavender oil on your feet, to help keep you grounded. Blow out the blue votive, and wave the smoke over your head. You are now aura cleansed.

Set up an altar with the spell ingredients. Place the jasmine, rose buds and hibiscus in the wood box together, and put the yarrow in the charm bag. Begin anointing the yin yang candle and the crystals with ylang ylang oil. Place the pyramid in the wood box, and bury it under the flowers. Place the jasper worry stone in the charm bag with the yarrow.

Now sit for a few minutes, to calm and clear your mind. When you are ready, light the yin/yang candle, and begin repeating this incantation:

what's done is done
it's over
what was
is buried in the past
I release my lover from my heart
and burn my pain to ashes

Keep repeating this while you write down all your feelings about your lover and your break up. Write down *everything*,
good, bad and indifferent.

When you have everything down, sprinkle some frankincense over the charcoal, and touch your written feelings to the candle flame. Keep repeating the incantation until the written words are entirely burnt to ashes. Sweep the ashes into the box with the amethyst pyramid, and close the lid. Place the charm bag on top of the box. Rub a few drops of ylang ylang oil on your palms, and your temples. Now envelope the box and charm bag with your hands, radiating energy into them while repeating:

like the Phoenix from it's ashes
love arises, renewed and reborn
as free as a bird
as fresh as a flower
as fragrant as incensed air
my love is reborn

Charge the stones until your energy is dissipated. Place the box somewhere near the center of your living room or bedroom, so that the energy of the pyramid can act absorb and dissipate the sorrow, and lighten the atmosphere.

Keep the worry stone charm bag with you, and if you feel overwhelmed with sadness or anger, rub the stone with your thumb until the feelings have dissipated. Also, keep the ylang ylang oil with you, using it to anoint the worry stone daily. You can also use it as an aromatherapy oil, as well as smelling the herbs in the charm bag.

Always send good thoughts to your love- not clingy, desperate thoughts, but honest thoughts for that person's
happiness and well being. You can sprinkle the pyramid and wood box every other day with lavender oil, to keep it, and the atmosphere of your home, purified.

Before we get to the Money spells, a few words on 'Prosperity'
What do you think prosperity is? Do you simply think it's another word for rich? Or do you understand the word "prosper" as a synonym for thrive, flower, prevail, to blossom? Do you see prosperity in terms of growth?

The first thing you need to do is stop *thinking* about money! Let go of 'mental metaphysics' - start *feeling* about it. Feeling plays the largest role in manifesting - what you put your *emotions* to, (not your thoughts) is where your energy is flowing, and what your energy is focused on will eventually come your way!

Try this- take out the crispest, cleanest, newest bill in your wallet right now... and smell it! *I want you to memorize the sweet smell of money!* Our memories operate in all our senses, and the sense of smell is a powerful one. Every time you pay for something, smell a bill, and think to yourself "Unlimited Wealth", and pass it along to the next person!

(For a truly powerful and deep prosperity transformation, go to www.get-rich-mp3-download.com)

Money Attraction Spell

You will need:

A seven knob green candle

Green rutilated quartz point massager

Green charm bag

Sea Salt

Sage

Basil

Chamomile

Pennyroyal

Moss

Sage smudge

Pine oil

Cedar oil

Dollar bill and coins

Wooden box

Seven days before the Full Moon, anoint the candle with pine oil. Light it, and fill the wood box with sea salt. Place the quartz crystal in the box, and bury it in the sea salt, to purify its energy. In the green charm bag, place the dollar and coins along with the herbs, to charge the herbs with money power. Now, smudge the room, the spell ingredients, and yourself. Burn the candle down one knob. Burn one knob of the candle every night.

On the evening before the Full Moon, transfer the crystal from the salt to the charm bag. Use the salt to make the Prosperity Bath salts- sprinkle with cedar oil, and mix with chamomile flowers.

On the night of the Full Moon, draw a hot bath with the prosperity bath salts. Light the last knob of the candle. Bathe, and repeat this incantation:

prosperity infuses my being

After the bath, remove the crystal from the charm bag, and massage your body with it, particularly the back of your legs. Smudge the area afterwards. Also massage in a few drops of the cedar oil into the backs of your legs. Keep the crystal stored in the charm bag with the herbs and money, and carry it as a charm.

Money Tree Prosperity Spell
You will need:
Green votive candles
Brown votive candle
A miniature orange or kumquat tree
(if you have a "brown thumb", try an aloe vera)
Spring water
Plant food
Pine incense
Pine oil
Sage
Basil
Pennyroyal
Moss
Large terra cotta pot
A dollar bill

On the evening of the Full Moon, set up an area where you can leave the ceremonial items undisturbed, overnight. Place your plant in the center of it. Contemplate this plant, and with sincerity, repeat this Earth prayer:

I am grounded and rooted firmly in the earth, like this plant. I draw nourishing energy from the Earth, the Sun, the Air, and Water, like this plant. The elements of life sustain me.

Add the recommended amount of plant food to the spring water, and say this Water prayer:

Water, giver of life, oasis in the desert, quench my thirst. Always moving, always flowing, like a great river, a gentle stream, like the waves of the ocean, I will not grow stagnant. I ask the powers that guide and protect me to bless this offering.

Place this water to the left of your plant. Inside the pot, with a permanent marker, write this incantation:

I am a living, growing being, just like this plant. Always changing, ever evolving, I reach for the sky, yet remain rooted firmly in the Earth. I nourish and nurture this plant, the symbol of my prosperity, and in return, the Universe nourishes and nurtures me. Every day this plant grows a bigger, a greener, more lush, and soon it will blossom and bear fruit, just as my life will blossom, and bear the fruit of prosperity.

Make sure you get a pot big enough to write all this! Now take the herbs sprinkle it with a few drops of pine oil, and mix them together into a potpourri. Place this in your terra cotta pot, and put it to the right of your plant.

Now, use a few drops of pine oil to dress the candles. You can rub a little on your temples, too. Place the brown candle to the left of the plant, and the green candle to the right. As you light them, say the Fire prayer:

Candle flame, element of fire, consume the poverty I feel in my heart. Transform my heart into a fertile field (the brown candle) in which a new life of abundance will grow.

Now, imagine yourself to be a tree, roots reaching far into the Earth, branches reaching high, high into the sky, feel yourself growing. When you feel really strong and solid, repeat the incantation you wrote in the pot. Say it over until you feel satisfied, then light two sticks of incense, one in each candle. Then say the Air prayer:

On a gentle breeze, a strong wind, in the still warm air of summer, my hopes, prayers and dreams rise like a fragrant smoke. Like the Gods, the element of Air is everywhere, unseen but real. It connects and sustains all life, and with every breath I take, I am more deeply woven into the fabric of the world. My breath is my connection to the natural abundance and goodness of the Earth, it is my constant and sustaining prayer.

Now, on the Front of the dollar bill, write your name. On the back write the word ABUNDANCE. Set this in the center, right in front of your plant.

Feel finished with this ritual, and go out for a long walk. If you can not walk far, go to a movie, a cafe, just get out into the world. If you go out to eat, leave the waitress a nice big tip! The point is, get out of your house, get out of yourself, and take a look around with new eyes! See the world as a place where you belong, a place full of opportunities.

In the morning, after you've had breakfast and feel awake, it will be time to finish by transplanting your plant to its new pot. Start by removing the potpourri, and place it in a bowl or basket somewhere where it will scent your environment. Then place a few inches of soil on the bottom of the pot, and place the dollar bill on top of that. Then put in the plant. Say this:
As the roots of this plant grow through this symbol of prosperity, so shall my roots reach into the abundant heart of the Earth.

Place your plant in a nice, warm sunny place. Know that as it grows, little by little, so will the abundance in your life. Be patient, it wont happen over night. DO NOT OBSESS ON THE SPELL! Once you are done, it is done. You can keep it in the back of your mind, while you keep your eyes open for opportunities. Be thankful for even the smallest gift you might receive.

On a weekly basis, as you water the plant, repeat the incantation to yourself. Take this time to make sure the plant is healthy and give it any extra care it needs.

If your plant dies, don't worry or take it as a bad omen! Its possible the plant has absorbed a lot of negativity, so you should re-do the ritual with a new plant, which more than likely will do better.

Find a Job Spell
You will need:
Green candle
Frankincense incense
Frankincense oil
Quartz crystal
Sea salt
Galangal root
Sage
Sage smudge
Green charm bag
Pen and paper

The night before the New Moon, store the crystal in the sea salt, to purify its energy.

On the night of the New Moon, anoint the candle with frankincense oil. Light it, then use this flame to light the smudge. Smudge yourself and your aura, while repeating this incantation:

I am purified
and magnetized
with the power
to attract

the job of my dreams

Now, by the light of the candle, write down *everything* you want in a job, or to happen with your present job- salary, hours, location, and more importantly, the type of people you want to be around, and the sort of work atmosphere you wish to be in- casual, formal, professional, friendly, etc.

When you are done, rub the herbs into the paper, then carefully fold the herbs into the paper, like a little envelope. Place the quartz crystal in with the herbs, while repeating:

my job is signed and sealed to me
contentment, honor, prosperity

Drip some candle wax to seal this envelope, and slip it into the green velvet charm bag. Smudge yourself and the room again, and carefully smudge the leftover salt.

Whenever you go to a job interview, cast a pinch of this salt over your left shoulder. Or, sprinkle it around your current workplace. Keep the charm with you at all times.

Wishing Well Spell

You will need:
A white floating candle
A bowl, preferably silver
One big pinch chamomile flowers
Cedar oil
Coins

On the evening of the full moon, preferably near a window that will allow moonlight to shine in, fill the silver bowl with water. Drop in the coins while contemplating your desire, and say this prayer:

Mother Moon
Deities of the deep well of my being

Hear my prayer
And grant my desire

Sprinkle the chamomile flowers onto the water, as an offering to the deities of water. Anoint the candle with cedar oil, and light it. Let it float in the silver bowlful of water til morning. You can simply throw away the remains of the candle, discard the water and chamomile outside, under a bush or tree, and pocket the change!

Find a New Home Spell
You will need:
Yin/yang shaped candle
Nag champa incense
Wooden box
Amethyst egg
Red rose buds
Rose hips
Green velvet charm bag
Patchouli oil
Paper and pen

On the night of the New Moon, anoint the yin yang candle with patchouli oil. Light the candle, and from the candle, light two sticks of incense.

Hold the amethyst egg between your palms, in a prayer position, and meditate on the type of home you want. When you have it completely visualized- not only the floor plan, price and location, also the neighbors, neighborhood, safety, etc- write it all down.

Next, pour the herbs on the paper and say, with the egg folded in your hands:

my home, my nest
I plant the seed
the egg is formed
a new place
for me

Repeat this until it feels 'set'. Sweep half of the herbs into the wood box, and place the amethyst egg into it. Fold the paper, and place it into the charm bag with the rest of the herbs. Keep this with you, especially when you are out and about- it will act as a beacon, or homing device, for your new home. Place the wood box with the amethyst egg in your present home, to also attract what you desire.

Keep the Peace
You will need:
Yin/yang shaped candle
Mortar and pestle
Charm bag or box
Silver bowl
Black cloth
Sea salt
Shiva lingam stone (if unavailable, an amethyst or quartz egg)
Fennel seed
Flax seed
Rose buds
Rose oil

The evening before the ritual, immerse the lingam stone in the dry sea salt, to clarify and purify its vibration.

On the evening of the Full Moon, anoint the candle thoroughly with the rose oil, repeating this incantation:

*as within the heart
so within these walls
peace and harmony preside
on the inside*

By the light of the candle, grind the herbs into a fine powder in the mortar and pestle, repeating:

*I invoke the spirit
of harmony
to release from the essence of these herbs
the power to protect*

When the herbs are thoroughly ground, place them in the silver bowl with the lingam stone, and cover it with the black cloth. Leave it overnight in a safe place. The next day, sprinkle the corners of your home and/or office with the herbs, paying particular attention to places where people gather the most. Keep the stone in the charm box or bag, under your bed or mattress, or if the problems are mostly a work, keep it hidden in your desk.

Remember, the practice of meditation and the integrity of your aura and energy flow provide the best protection on a daily basis. Spellwork should only be necessary when under a deliberate psychic attack, or if negative spirits have become attracted to you.

Protection Spell
You will need:
Black cat shaped candle
Pair of white candles
Myrrh resin
Charcoal burner
Shiva lingam stone (or quartz or obsidian egg or sphere)
Lemon oil
Myrrh oil

Frankincense oil
Dandelion root
Rose hips
Fennel seed
Blessed thistle

Mix the dandelion and rose hips, and draw a line with it down the center of your altar. Next, mix the fennel and blessed thistle, and draw another line, crossing the first. Anoint the black cat candle with lemon oil, and set it at the top of the cross. Anoint one white candle with myrrh, and set it on the right arm of the cross. Anoint the other with frankincense, and set it at the left arm of the cross. Place the Shiva lingam stone at the center. This drives a symbolic wedge into your enemy's power. Call your guardian angel or other protector spirit into the cat candle. Ask the spirit guides to supercharge the lingam with protective powers. Light the candles and the charcoal, burn the myrrh resin, and say this incantation:

unwanted spirits I call to thee
I call thee into the light
guardian spirits I call to thee
I call thee to the fight
herb and candle burn away
lingam stone will clear the way
go back to where you need to stay
leave my home, just go away

While the candles, herbs and stone aid your guardian spirit in trapping the unwanted spirit or influence, take a bath, using a few drops each of the essential oils. Completely release any tension and fear, and know the forces of good will protect you.

Let the candles burn down completely. Take the old wax, and the herbs, and cast them into the charcoal burner, letting them all burn completely. Take the ashes, and cast them into the ocean, or a river, stream or canal. Keep the lingam stone in a high place, near the center of your home, for further protection.

Mirror Protection Spell

You will need:
A small new mirror
A permanent marker pen
Sea salt
Sage smudge
Red thread
A glass Eye shaped bead or charm

This spell is best suited for protection against specific people projecting negativity or aggression your way.

First cleanse the mirror by rubbing it gently with the dry sea salt. Repeat this:

I cleanse this mirror to reflect back true to the source.
As I cleanse this mirror, I cleanse my intention.

It is important to not feel angry, desperate or defensive while doing this; simply remain focused on cleansing your own soul of negativity, and working into the mirror a sense of objectivity and truth.

Next, rub the glass Eye bead or charm with salt, while whispering to it:

Watch for me, my psychic eye, my friend, my ally
Alert me of harm, of malicious games,
Warn me of those who work against me
I Bless you, and trust you as my ally and friend

If your mirror is double sided, with one magnifying side, write this around in a spiral on the *plain* side with the permanent marker:

Reflect back the negativity projected by (insert the persons name, if you know it, or just say, 'those who work against me') back to them. Let any harm or malicious intent go back to it's source.

You may also write the names and/or symbols of your personal protection deities and angels on the mirror, to invoke their protection. The archangel Michael is a good choice. This is especially effective if your mirror has a magnifying side; it is best to "magnify" the protective qualities of your personal deities, rather than magnifying the reflection of negativity. You just want to send back what is being projected 'as is'- sending it back magnified would violate the Threefold Law and create Bad Karma for you!

Next, you can tie the glass Eye to the mirror with the red thread, while saying this:

Aid this magick mirror with your insight.

Or, if you can hide the Eye someplace where your adversary frequents (such as near his or her desk at the office, near a school locker, near their home) place the glass Eye there, telling it:

Watch what (insert name) does, and let me know.
Watch what (insert name) does, and help the mirror in it's task

The final step is to hang the mirror in a window of your home. It can be a window facing the direction the negativity is coming from, or the window of the room in your house you most identify with. You can also place it where the 'psychic attack' is most likely to occur; you can hide it in your desk or locker if the person who is perpetrating the psychic attack is at work or school.

Prosperity Bath Salts- Mix one cup sea salt or Epsom salts with ¼ cup chamomile flowers. Sprinkle with about 20 drops of cedar oil while stirring. Let it sit for at least an hour, to absorb the fragrance.

Love Bath Salts- Mix one cup sea salt or Epsom salts with ¼ cup lavender or rose petals (your choice). Sprinkle with about 20 drops of rose or lavender oil. Let it sit for at least an hour, to absorb the fragrance.

If you can't find the exact ingredients for any of these spells, feel free to use the information in this book to find substitutes and improvise. Magick is all about creativity! And remember-

Mind the Threefold Law you should
Three times Bad and Three times Good

Eight words the Wiccan Rede fulfill
An ye Harm None, Do What ye Will.

We hope this book has been helpful- it is primarily a book for quick reference, full of useful knowledge and techniques to draw upon when you need it most. If you desire to know more about any subject concerning magick or metaphysics, you are wholeheartedly encouraged to read more! The world of the mind, metaphysics and magick are endlessly fascinating. Knowledge is power, and there are many great authors, both old and new, Wiccan and otherwise, who can point the way on your personal path to self discovery, magick, empowerment and enlightenment!

Come visit us on the world wide web!

Wejee's Free Psychic Readings
www.wejees.net

Wejee's Metaphysical Superstore
For more than 2,000 spirit filled herbs, oils, crystals, books, charms, music, jewelry, altar items and much more!
www.wejees.com

The Science of Getting Rich, updated for the 21st Century
With subliminal and self hypnosis downloads
www.get-rich-mp3-download.com

)O(

Raven Starhawk Cunningham is a hereditary witch, and learned an eclectic blend of metaphysics and magick from her innovative and very popular and magickal parents. She received a fine arts education at Arizona State University, and went on to earn a degree in Metaphysics. She grew up in close proximity to the spiritual center of Sedona, and is blessed to be currently living and working on the site of a Vortex, as a professional, practicing Eclectic Wiccan White Witch.

Dr. Jane Ma'ati Smith C.Hyp. Msc.D. is a spiritual counselor who studied for her Bachelor of Arts degree at Arizona State University, and went on to receive a doctorate in Metaphysical Science. She studied hypnosis with Dr. John Kappas, and is a certified graduate of the Hypnosis Motivation Institute, and also a Sound Energy Practitioner and a Vibrational Reiki Master. She is a member of American MENSA, and a qualified mental health professional actively working in the state of California.

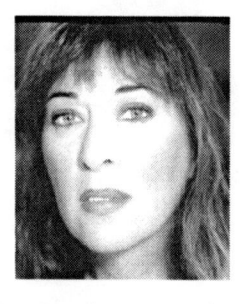

For all of your magickal, mystical, and metaphysical needs and desires, visit Wejee's Metaphsyical Superstore at
www.wejees.com